"The clock showed four and twenty-five.....
when England dreamt itself alive....."

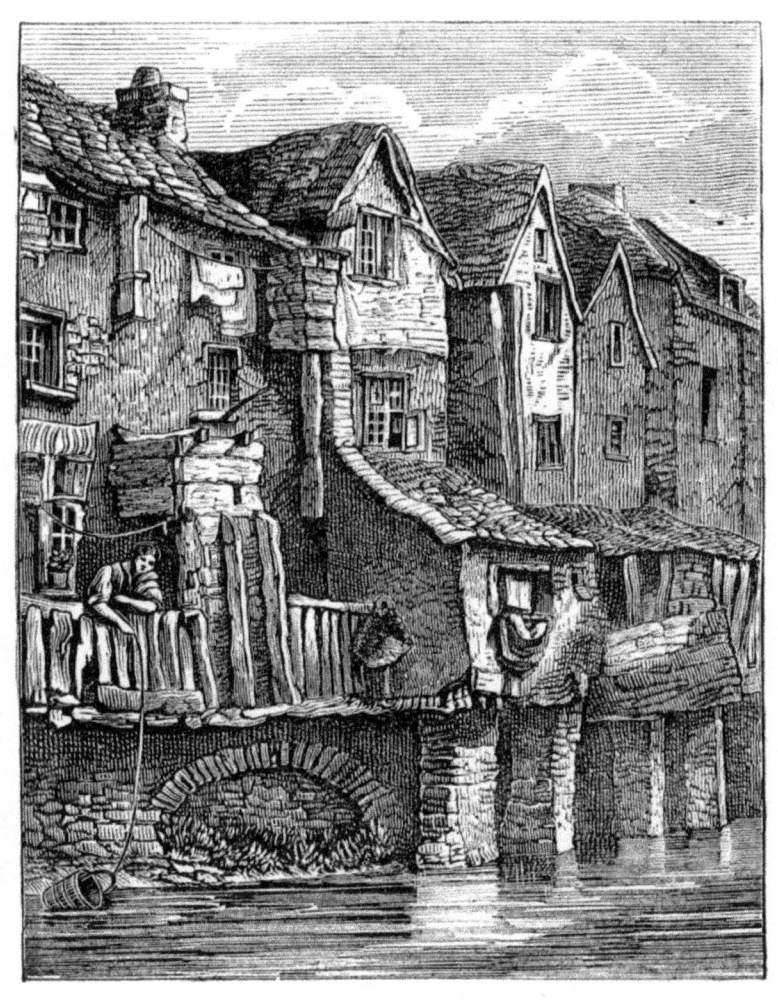

PARADISE CON-DEMed

........Further rants and ramblings of a Bristolian cynic

DARREN HURLEY

First published by Darren Hurley in 2011
Copyright © Darren Hurley 2011

The right of Darren Hurley to be identified as the author of this work has been asserted by him in accordance with the Copyright, Designs and Patents Act, 1988.

All rights reserved. No part of this book may be reproduced in any form or by any electronic or mechanical means, including information storage and retrieval systems, without written permission from the publisher or author, except in the case of a reviewer, who may quote brief passages embodied in critical articles or in a review.

Copyright text: Darren Hurley

Cover design by the author in collaboration with lulu.com.

Printed and bound by Lulu in 2011.

ISBN: 978-0-9566263-1-8

Darren Hurley and Sugary Tea Publications

Every effort has been made to acknowledge the appropriate copyright holders.

Acknowledgement to all known authors of copyright-free images are listed at the back of this book.

Contact author at darrenhurley27@talktalk.net

www.darrenhurleysparadisepoems.com

"The aim of science is to make difficult things understandable in a simpler way; the aim of poetry is to state simple things in an incomprehensible way."

Paul Dirac

*For Bob Isaacs, a true gentleman and a kindred spirit –
a man with many warm words of wisdom and
encouragement.........*

Thanks also to Bet Elland for words of encouragement..........

Apologies to 'Works Management', on whose premises a surprising amount of this material was written..........

"THERE IS *NO* MONEY LEFT.....

we have *nothing* more to give....."

FOREWARD - "Author's woe"

The Poet's life's a sorry one,
as I can say, it's not much fun -
I sweat and toil until I curse,
to come up with some cracking verse.....

Pyjama-clad, I lay in bed
and scribble down what's in my head –
I sometimes type into my phone,
my *only* use of *'dog and bone'!*

Now even when I'm on the bog,
poetic thoughts are in my 'nog,
so if I've got no pad, no "scroll",
gets written on the toilet roll!

Been working round the clock to find
the formula that needs designed,
to satisfy the people's thirst
for topics, that are inter-versed

And all for *what?* I'm *not* a bore,
yet find the wolves are at my door –
a stack of bills that lay unpaid,
my dreams of fame and fortune fade......

The first book that I wrote last year,
would sell a *'mill'* - the shelves would clear –
at least, that was the line I got,
when I was in 'financial spot'

Imagine how my blood turned cold,
when I found only *thirteen* sold!
The manager who runs my bank
is going mad, I've drawn a blank!

He's put the pressure back on me,
to print the next successfully –
in other words, *this book* you hold,
it needs to strike proverbial gold.....

Referring back, again – last year,
to debut books and 'lack of cheer' –
(I mean the volume titled *"Glossed"*,
which purposely, had rhymed with *"Lost"*) –

Well in that book, I sort of said
there would be *more* rhymes from my head –
in other words, on me, depend -
(*'to be continued'* - at the end)

Result of which, you see is *this* –
the *second* of poetic bliss (!) -
six months of observations when
the year was still two thousand-ten

I've written these at *faster* rate
than last year, though I can relate -
a year ago, well, I was *'green'*,
but twelve months on, I'm extra *mean!*

Let me remind you, as I craft,
the state of my big overdraft -
the heat is on for me to sell,
so *fingers crossed*, and time will tell.....

I work my fingers to the bone
(and text my verse into the phone) –
the aim, to bring poetic class
unto the Bristol public mass.....

I write these things, though it's a pain,
my only purpose – *"Entertain"*
So if you don't give me 'the bird',
you never know, might be a *third*........

Oh – I forgot.....

"Bristolians – *'The Matthew'* sails..........roll up for Parliament!!
We'll hand in our petition, stating *they're* incompetent!
It's true, our ship's seen *better* days - been stripped down to it's guts -
so sad, *another* victim of these *wretched* spending cuts!!"

The Poems.....   Turn to page.....

1. Fingers crossed..1

2. Three cheers for Mr Chatterton......................................3

3. Won't you come and dine with me - again (and again)?................6

4. Our Noble Leader (or, 'An Address to King Dave') 8

5. Our Noble Deputy (or, 'An Address to Mr Clegg')...............11

6. Ireland - her time in rhyme (Part One)..............................13

7. Life is s**t at forty...18

8. A license to chill...21

9. Three cheers for Mr Davy...25

10. Lidl Britain...27

11. I is a British teenager 30

12. Ireland - her time in rhyme (Part Two)............................32

13. A doodle door...37

14. Greetings from Dorset ('Postcard to a pensioner')...........38

15. Charmouth beach..40

16. Ode to a Nightingale..41

17. Ode to a Sky Lark..42

18. Ireland - her time in rhyme (Part Three).........................43

19. A Dublin text message..48

20. Life in the money factory...49

21. Lady Molyneaux 51

22. Friday's child...53

23. "I'm only here to shop!"..54

24. A letter to my leader...57

25. Ireland – her time in rhyme (Part Four)..........................60

26. Three cheers for Mr Archibald......................................65

27. Ode to the Robin...68

28. Ode to our beautiful river..70

29. "Tart FM"..71

30. The Ten Commandments...73

31. Ireland – her time in rhyme (Part Five)..........................75

32. Let's throw an egg at Mr Clegg....................................80

33. 4:25pm (A dream) #...81

34. Poem for the Polish / Poemat dla Polakow..................83

35. Three cheers for Mr Dirac..85

36. Two Georges..87

37. The Guy Fawkes Dilemma (1605)................................88

38. Ireland – her time in rhyme (Part Six)...........................90

39. "There's gonna be a riot!!"..95

40. Fly the flags – blow the bugles!...................................97

41. Scandal Days..99

42. Man's pest friend..106

43. Five have an awfully spiffing time...............................108

44. Cable under the table (A "Fable")..............................120

45. The road to Weston Pier..121

46. Ireland – her time in rhyme (Part Seven)...................122

47. How do you solve a problem like Korea?....................130

48. People in Europe...133

49. Winston's war chant...135

(The Tyrants Trilogy)

50. Napoleon's Diary..137

51. Mine Campf..150

52. My little-read book..155

53. Headley Park (I remember, I remember)....................158

54. An extra little star...161

"Other things"..163

.........<u>Thursday April 29th 2010</u>

....and God did say

he'd send a *scourge*,

a pestilence would

thus emerge -

so if you think

we've had it bad,

you *will* cry

out for

what

we

had!

"**Fingers crossed.....**"   Friday May 7th 2010

"The fall-out from the Election".....

Fingers crossed, and hold your nose
cuz' where we're going, no-one knows....
now Britain's landed in the dung –
the Parliamentary House is hung
Will Davy do a deal with Nick?
The very thought – it makes me sick!
Or Clegg is shaking Gordon's hand?
- to keep them masters of the land......(?)

Fingers crossed, and hold your breath
we're going on a dance of death –
I hope and will with all I've got
the Liberals back the Labour lot...
Cuz' while the Tory vote has grown,
they *ain't* enough to "go alone" –
so Davy's hiding in his den,
with *NOT* enough for "Number 10"

Fingers crossed, and say a prayer
it looks as if we've got a pair –
a partnership to sort the mess,
to calm the economic stress

I hope you're feeling quite perplexed,
for we all know what's coming next –
all Public things stripped to the bone,
the biggest cuts we've ever known.....

Now fingers crossed, and hold on tight –
Brown's going now, without a fight
No point in shedding tears galore,
now this is what *YOU* voted for!
It's too late now, no time for *"If's"* –
this country's going off the cliffs...
and too late now, no time for *"But's"* –
sit tight, here come the spending cuts.....

So fingers crossed, and close your eyes –
the pre-election spin – all lies!
Both manifesto's ripped in two,
they're making joined-up plans anew
Sworn enemies, just five days past –
now "love is here", but will it last?
All Party roots have come un-stemmed,
now Britain's future is *Con-Dem*ed!

*Written over the course of Friday May 7th to Tuesday May 11th 2010.

"Three cheers for Mr Chatterton" Thursday May 13th 2010

"He was a decent poet, oh it's really such a shame –
cuz' forging's what he's known for, and it's how he made his
name".....

Three cheers for Mr Chatterton!
- and streets named after he.....
who "found" a book of history,
turned out, *his* forgery!
He claimed he got the document
(a type of manuscript) –
within St Mary Redcliffe Church,
a lie, which later slipped.....

Young Thomas was a poet boy,
a nipper – not eighteen!
But when his tale was shown a fib,
he found that times were lean.....
So travelled to the capital,
(that's London) – seeking fame –
but fortune slow.....and income low,
his forging was to blame.....

His reputation ever-scarred,
he had a ghastly job –
to pay his rent and water bill,
on half a dozen 'bob'.....
Alas, poor Thomas lost his way,
so penned a sorry note –
then took a glass with poison in,
and tipped it down his throat!

Now, when I grace St Mary's pews,
I think *"Hallo there, Tom!*
You fooled so many Bristol folk,
yet did it with aplomb!
Although you were a lying hound,
it was with impish charm –
a wonder that you pulled it off,
before you found alarm".....

"I know you were a lonely boy
who never had a dad -
imagination was your crime,
a thing that's hardly bad.....
I'm sorry that you never grew,
matured, and found a wife –
poor Tommy, how I grieve for you,
and your poetic life".....

The death of Chatterton

St Mary Redcliffe, Bristol

"Won't you come and dine with me - again (and again)?"
Sunday May 16th 2010

"I want to taste what you've to eat.....so I can carp, and moan, and bleat".....

There's programmes on our TV screens,
I'd say they're on too much –
not every month, nor every week,
but every *DAY* as such!
Included, there's this cooking thing,
that's always blinkin' ON!
It's a televisual echo,
it's a culinary con!

Amidst the busy kitchen scenes
(the host so busy, cooks) –
it seems to me, that outside
there's a bunch of sneaky crooks!
Intruding in her bedroom,
now they're rifling through her drawers,
then they're opening up the wardrobe
and they look behind the doors!

They'll bitch about the clothes she's got,
next look upon her walls –
then slag off all her pictures too,
and say *"they're utter balls!"*
Now if you think it's finished there,
the end of being rude –
before you know, they're chauffeured home
and moaning at her food!

I'd not complain, or have my say,
but this is on *THREE TIMES A DAY!*
So every time I channel-flick –
it's on *AGAIN*....a nasty trick!
So how do they expect to get
a decent score(?), and so I bet –
they've got their viewers 'on the snore',
those cheeky pups at Channel Four!

"Our Noble Captain (Or, 'An Address to King Dave')"
Friday June 18th 2010

"The annual letter sent to Downing Street....this year, bearing a new name"......

King Dave! Your Royal Eton pup!
How very fast, you've slithered up
the greasy pole, which held no fear –
you've hit the top, yet from the rear!
Your Tory Party looked at Blair
and thought it was a tad unfair –
"A Tony clone is needed here",
then flamin' Nora, *YOU* appear!

A question, for your regal snout
(you love to show what you're about!)
Why are you keen to cover up
your schooldays as an '*Eton pup*'?
Your silver spoon did get you far,
it put you on a Royal par –
that public school of high repute,
oh, Eton days were such a hoot!

Three things, I think you seek to hide –
(as yet, it seems you've not replied?)
your boyish days, I've mentioned Dave.....
at Oxford, *DID* you mis-behave?
Ah, *"Bullingdon's"* elitist club –
that upper *crust-ic*, royal "pub",
for champagne-swilling Tory twits
and restaurant-trashing Eton gits.....

And what's all this, in '92 –
"Black Wednesday", partly down to you?
The E.R.M. and all that mess,
which gave the country much distress?
Your Chancellor, he got the boot,
(Lord Norman, he of ill-repute) –
yet *now* I find, to be precise,
from YOU, he took his c—p advice!

Oh goodness Dave, I never knew –
you caused our economic stew!
Why is it that you never said (?) –
'cuz you blamed old Lamont instead?
Yet Dave, in you we hold our trust
to stop the country going bust,
your Georgy-boy's a massive job
(that's Osborne, fellow Eton snob)

But Davy, do you hear "the street"?
Know WHY the working classes bleat (?) –
when you were raised an "upper ass"
protected by the middle-class?
What will you say, 'cept "If" or "But" (?),
cuz' workers are the ones you'll cut,
when Georgy-porgy breaks the news
of Comprehensive cash reviews.....

We're in a mess, our country's broke,
your Manifesto's up in smoke –
your *'Con-Dem'* partners, awkward sit.....
uncomfortable with most of it
Oh goodness, how you need a "Ken",
to move in next to 'Number Ten' –
I'm sure that Clarke could sort it out,
(that's use our cash, whilst spending nowt)

And though you'll blame the Labour lot,
opinion polls won't give a jot –
cuz' when you start the Public purge,
your ratings sure *WON'T* see a surge!
I know you'd like to "hug a hood",
but don't think that will do much good,
so Davy boy, it won't be fun –
oh Mr Cam, what CAN be done??

"Our Noble Deputy (or, 'An Address to Mr Clegg')"
Tuesday June 22nd 2010

"Budget Day in Britain".........

Oh Mr Nick! You look so glib.....
my goodness me, you've told a fib!
I know that look, from whence it stems –
it's links with parties called *'Fib Dems'*!
Election time, not long ago,
great poster things you had on show!
Now let me think, *what* did I see?
Ah – "*Stop the rise in V.A.T!*"

'Twas April / May – "*oh, look at me!
I am the saint on YOUR T.V. –
no baggage do I bring with me,
I've come to set the Nation free!
Now please don't trust the 'other two',
they've put this country in the stew –
these 'two old parties' make me sick,
now here's the thing – 'Agree with Nick!'*

DO NOT trust that 'Eton pup' –
he'll go and put your taxes up!"
But Mr Clegg, what do I find –
you've left that promise well behind?
And you did go and make a pact –
your voters, spun a lie in fact,
'*New Politics*', that's what *you* said –
and *now* you've sold your souls instead!

Oh Mr Nick, what *have* you done?
The biggest con under the sun!
Now all I ever hear is jeers –
your Party's set back fifty years....
Cuz' eighty years it's taken you,
to come *this* far – now down the loo!
Your membership looks on in vain –
they'll *NEVER* vote for you again!

Oh Mr Nick – you're *NOT* a saint!
You *were* in March, but *now* you ain't!
And never will we trust the *Lib*s,
when all they ever tell is fibs!
So now you're Britain's "*Number Two*",
well, "hip-hip-hip"........that's great for you,
but Mr Nick, take note I pray –
your '*Democrats*' have had their day!

So come Election time one May,
some sunny, distant time away.....
your scheme to play with boys in blue
won't go away, but turn on you....
Oh Mr Clegg, your plan so dumb
will come and bite you on the bum...
enjoy it while you can, oh Nick –
now can't you see how time does tick.........

"Ireland – her time in rhyme (Part One)"
Sunday June 27th 2010

"Irish.........Catholic.........Protestants – you haven't got a clue?
The I.R.A..........King Billy – now it's all explained for you!"
(500BC – AD 1540)

"St Patrick was an Irishman" –
WHOEVER told you that?
About as Irish as a
good old English cricket bat!
Oh yes, he came to visit,
but the legends, they are fakes –
"he came to spread the word of God
and banished all the snakes" (??)

Yet don't forget the Celtic folk
who travelled far and wide -
then set up camp on *Erin's Isle,*
now home to Gaelic pride!
Their culture, language, customs, sports,
were things, destined to stay –
from right back *then*, in olden times,
until the I.R.A.!

Now Ireland *did* go Catholic,
so of that I can't deny –
just like her cousin *Eng-er-land*,
on whom she did rely.....
But islanders are funny things,
and feelings do grow cold,
see they crave for independence
and they simply *WON'T* be told!

Cuz', being cast away from England
by a little pond –
breeds thoughts of self-importance
and makes feelings grow UN-fond!
So it did come to be, back then
that tension festered deep,
as an Anglo-Irish *"Cold War"*
did begin to slowly creep.....

Now Brian Boru was a King,
'twas from the Irish south –
who wanted proof he was "the deal",
not just a motor-mouth!
So sought he to impose his will
on all the little clans,
with this *"Emperor of Ireland"* tag
the centre of his plans.....

He also fought to unify
the leaders of the land –
so better-placed to nullify
the Viking upper-hand!
See, Danish were the rage back then,
invasion was their game –
but Brian sought to tone it down,
and end in all but name

Remembered as a hero
in near every Irish town –
in battle, Brian lost his life,
they cut and slew him down
Uneasy peace with England,
this did follow for a time –
but peace ain't everlasting,
as will show this little rhyme.....

Skip forward now, five hundred years –
(this history's full of holes!)
when good old Henry Tudor
had these re-producing goals!
"So what's all that to do with Irish lands?"
I hear you say –
*"I'm NOT interested in Henry
and his rolling in the hay!"*

Well.........

Oh Catherine of Aragon,
if you had only done
the decent thing, and bore
old Henry Tudor's little son....
cuz' then he got fed up with you,
decided you were *OUT* –
(too interested in other girls,
and putting it about!)

A *"wild rover"* he would be,
that Henry number eight –
he fell in love with French girls
and this got him in a state!
Our Kingdom, it was Catholic then,
including Ireland too –
a problem for old Henry
when he wanted *"Wifey Two"!*

If Henry wanted Anne Boleyn,
he needed a divorce –
his Holiness the Pope would show him
little in remorse.....
See, England being Catholic,
drew it's blessings from the Pope –
so Henry's big annulment (?),
well, he didn't have a hope!

Old Henry claimed (in bible terms)
his marriage must be cursed –
see, Katy – her of *"Aragon"*
had been his brother's FIRST!

But Arthur Tudor passed away,
left Katy all alone –
so Henry did the decent thing
and took her for his own!

But when she couldn't give the heir
that good old Henry craved –
he thought, *"I'll have that Anne Boleyn,
my Kingdom MUST be saved!"*
Yet what to do, when Clement
(that's the Pope!) won't grant divorce?
Thought Henry, *"Does this problem
have the answer at it's source?"*

*"This Catholic thing, get rid of it –
who needs the ruddy Pope?
Now if I had a church of MINE
I'm sure that I would cope!"*
The upshot of it all was this –
the Pope was cast away.......
and so was Katy Aragon,
came next, a wedding day!

So Henry married Anne Boleyn
and thought *"Well, that is THAT"* –
but Kate had been a Catholic *
and a wily Spanish cat.....
Now *this** is why the Pope refused
to grant a quick divorce -
yet Henry had re-married,
but there was no church of course!

So Henry looked at Protestants
and thought *"I fancy this!
I'll form a Church of England,
set the Catholics to abyss!
I'll put my very name to this,
to me, forever bound!
And as for all those monasteries,
I'll raze 'em to the ground!"*

But where did good old Ireland stand
amidst this scheme of things?
As Henry – King of Ireland too –
had *Irish* underlings......
So would this new religion
be accepted by the clans?
Oh dear, I think the English
might as well made *OTHER* plans!

TO BE CONTINUED.........

"Life is s**t at forty" Wednesday June 30th 2010

"So 'life will begin at..........FIFTY'??"

Yes, life is s**t when you're forty (and-a-bit),
it seems a con when you know you're getting on.....

Too old to play your football –

too old to go out dancing –

too old to hit the nightclubs –

too old to be on *Facebook* (??)

(Too old to be called "young man" *anymore, by anyone under the age of 75!)*

You're moaning at the telly.....

You're moaning at the radio.....

You're moaning at the papers.....

You're moaning at the weather.....

The buses......

and parking......

the sound of next door's barking!

You *know* your best days are behind –

the mirror shows you're extra-lined:-

those multi years, you'll *not* disguise,

because of crow's feet round your eyes.....

In fact:-

You know you're getting on a bit
if you can name the *ONLY* hit.....
.....by *"Yello"*, whom I can relate
achieved this feat in '88!

You know that you're a dinosaur
when Blackpool has become a bore,
I'll never take another ride
on that town's rollercoaster pride.....

You know you've reached a certain age
when Cowell makes you rant and rage –
you'd rather cut off all your toes
than cast a vote on 'Talent' shows.....

You know you're getting on in years
when *"Kiss FM's"* your height of fears –
you hear the sh**e that station plays
and feel you want to end your days.....

You *know* your life is shooting past –
Chris Moyles makes you feel aghast!
You'd rather hear (upon the snore)
"The Archers", them on 'number four' *

You know you're getting past your prime
when moaning that it's Christmas time –
too stingy when you're lashing out,
"they don't know what it's all about!!"

You know there's plenty 'on your clock'
when every 'morn, you feel a 'crock' -
those achy limbs and creaky bones,
oh, *how* the aged body groans!

You know that you're *'long in the tooth'*
when seems a lifetime from your youth –
the skill is gone, you've lost the knack,
it's far too late to get 'em back!

When you get old, I think you might
feel you've no stomach for the fight,
so if at first, you don't succeed,
then give it up, and just concede.....

*BBC Radio 4

"A license to chill"   Wednesday July 7th 2010

"For what THEY spend, with all our 'beans', there's RUBBISH on our TV screens - oh Logie Baird, you should have cared.....you're making all our eyes go squared!"

If Logie Baird had only known,
(inventing his TV) –
the *drivel* we would have to watch
when viewing after tea!

I'm sick of dancing, singing,
skating, *"Talent"*, cooks and co –
"control their fate" – *"eliminate"*,
"text who you want to go!"

Now Logie was a Scotsman,
so as such, would he applaud?
This *"flash your cash!"* – *"we want your stash!"*
 - I think he'd be appalled!

Now yes, I realise *Su Bo*,
(what a talent!!) is a Scot –
but Logie Baird, I'm telling you,
still wouldn't give a jot!

When Mr Cowell comes back on
our screens again, quite soon -
we'll see his ego – wallet *too* –
inflate like a balloon!

"*X Factor*"! - it's the show from hell,
those parasitic lice!
Not *only* crave your voting,
but they want your money *TWICE!*

"*So WHO goes now, it's down to YOU*",
blah blah – you *know* the biz' –
yet, *not enough* – cuz' by the end,
they want a 'ring-up' quiz!

So there you've got your A, B, C
three answers - you must pick -
insultingly, so easy -
they are questions for the thick!

It's money, greed, corruption,
and it makes me want to curse!
So *where* do all the profits go?
 - straight into Cowell's purse??

"*We're all in this together?*"
oh come on, that quote's a prank!
Try telling that to Simon,
whilst he's laughing to the bank!

Now all these shows are much the same,
celebs, or normal folk –
yet patterns say, there's always *one*,
we'll label him a joke!

Cuz' talking of contestants, well,
there's *always* '*weakest links*' –
but course, they're kept *in* long as poss',
creating public stinks.....

There's Sargent and there's Widdecombe*
blah blah, you want a list?
Those *Jedward* boys, and *Chico*,
now I'm sure you get the gist!

But we ain't fools, it's TV tools
and cons, nay, trickery –
'Publicity' – now *that's* the word,
they take the *'mickery'*!

ITV! Now *every* programme,
News and Weatherview –
it's sponsored by a *business*,
so, there's profit in *that* too!

Yet *BBC* and *ITV* – the lot,
they're *'on the make'* –
so "*text our quiz*" / "*Eliminate*",
it's all for profit's sake!

But when you strip the whole lot down
to "*PROGRAMMES*" ('member those?) -
subtract from all our TV screens,
the *trash*, it yonder goes.....

Removing all *"Celebrity"*,
"Reality", et al –
"Big Brother", cooking, property –
house-hunting with your pal......

Take *'X Factor'* and *'Strictly'* too,
then soap operas – what's *left*?
Now can't you see, for what we pay,
how quality's bereft?

Yet when it comes to budgets, well,
the *'Beeb'*, they want it *all* –
in other words, we pay our fee,
they fund their *'Digital'*!

That's fine and good, but *'Digital'*,
'on-line' and all *that* stuff –
is hardly used by *one and all*,
in fact, by not *enough*!

A-ha! So can't you see it now,
I've hit upon the clue?
They're taking *FROM* the *many*,
but they're spending *ON* the *few!*

So when it comes to license fees,
I'm telling you – we're mugs!
For us to pay this *willingly*,
we'd *have* to be on drugs!

***Reviewed in time** *(November 2010)* **so that I was in a position to include Ann Widdecombe's name in this poem – she was announced as a** *"Strictly"* **contestant in the Autumn.**

"Three cheers for Mr Davy"   Friday July 16th 2010

"Invented lamps and made some brass – he championed the laughing gas!"......

Three cheers for Mr Davy!
And lamps named after he...
(Invented for the Miners,
so that they could safely see!)
He learned to be a chemist
and he moved to Dowry Square -
(a little road in Hotwells,
not a stone's throw from *"The Bear"*)

Hooray for for Mr Davy!
(A Cornishman by birth) -
who travelled up to Bristol
for much merriment and mirth!
Then came the rich and famous,
for his house – they'd never pass,
cuz' he played with Nitrous Oxide
(which is known as 'laughing gas'!)

Now when I'm down a mine-shaft,
I do think *"oh, bless my soul!*
Humphry made the Miners safer,
when they're down here digging coal!
They hold his name in fond regard,
say 'Davy is our Champ!' –
so thank god for good old Humphry
and his good old Davy Lamp!"

"Lidl Britain"   Sunday August 1st 2010

"It's Osborne and his 'ginger Lib' – now are they spinning us a fib?"

The nasty Coalition cuts
will kick us Britons in the guts,
now England's broke, we've got no cash –
I'd turn to Labour in a flash.....
These people have no money cares,
this Cabinet of millionaires –
yet preach to us *"We've got no loot,*
we're going down the slashing route!"

Yes, Budget Britain's cutting deep,
this country's running on the cheap –
it's too late now, they won't relent,
these cuts of twenty-five percent!
Cost-cutting's what it's all about,
the M5 lights are going out.....
these "beauty spots", now I'm no kidder –
sold off to the highest bidder!

It seems there's nothing they won't do
to flush this country down the loo –
now Health and Education's stripped,
"it's not OUR fault!", we've heard the script.....

But England had a party when
New Labour was in Number Ten –
they over-spent, but times were great,
then Bankers left us to our fate.....

The Governmental limousine
is being axed, cuz' times are lean –
instead the *Con-Dem* team must go
around by bike, cuz' there's no dough!
Now if you think we're laughing stocks,
I'm finished NOT, there's further mocks –
they're flying cheapy, budget flights
for foreign trips and "seeing sights"!

Now Osborne says *"these cuts are right!
Oh trust in me, I'm rather bright!"*
So he engaged a ginger Lib
to filter through this sorry fib.....
Now Mr Alexander speaks
in echoes from the Tory beaks,
so how much lower can they sink(?) –
let's speculate on what they think:-

*"The Winter Fuel Allowance pays
our pensioners on chilly days –
we promised you it would remain,
(though paying out is such a pain!)
So we have hatched a sneaky plan
to raise the age for every "nan" –
you MUST be over sixty-five
to qualify to stay alive!"*

*"Free passes on our buses too!
(These pensioners don't have a clue!)
Now don't they realise what it costs
to Governments?(by whom they're bossed!)
We promised that these freebies stay,
so we shall narrow WHO we pay –
AGAIN, we want to "up" the age,
pre-65, we'll dis-engage!"*

*"Now WHO did Labour think they were
to treat the British pensioner?
By handing out these little gifts,
(it's causing us some major rifts!)
They even gave a free TV,
(by that, I mean a License Fee) –
to every OAP, a wad –
(when reached a certain age) – oh god!!"*

*"Our predecessor's been a pain,
they've left us with a nasty stain –
they showered gifts and gave away
these things – we can't afford to pay!
Now Schooling Funds and Benefits –
we're thinking, they are all THE PITS.....
and "Sure-Start" centres Labour gave,
we're trimming back, we need to save".....*

Now Liberal Democrat support
is plummeting, I can report –
cuz' they did state on V.A.T.
to put it up's a travesty!
But when they got in bed with Dave
they dug themselves an early grave –
*"Pooh! V.A.T.? I couldn't care.....
now ain't this great, let's power-share!"*

So what a scary ride we're on,
this FIB-eral Democratic *"Con"* –
the Treasury's a scam of course,
the *Con-Dems* double-headed horse.....
They're drinking from the Golden Cup,
with MP's wages going up,
now here's the icing on the cake –
they're on a paid-up three month break!

It's bound to end in tears of course,
this Coalition WILL divorce –
and *"Clegg-eron"* will soon break up
when Dave disowns his naughty pup!
So we'll be brave, we must stand firm,
they're "locked in" for a five-year term –
(another Bill they're sneaking through!),
so Britain's landed in the poo!

"I is a British teenager" Wednesday August 4th 2010

"How to interact with the average 21st Century adolescent"

i iz a Bristol teenager, my language is in TEXT –
my 'English' so distorted, you wont know wots' comin next!
b4 you gets all cross wiv me, you really needs to know –
I talks da language of the street, it's ezy, watch it flow!

I luvs 2 speak in lingo dat my folks wont understand –
cuz times is changed + textin talk iz rely in demand!
c, english is so *yesterday,* its krap an' out of date –
who wants to chat like shakespear, like its 1598?

i think theres textin websites, so dot.com an' check em out –
dats if you wanna speak in modern, nonsense, teeny spout.....
"r u on F.B.# ? Check me out, + add me as ur friend –
i'll copy / paste da link to you, + email, then i'll send".....

i dont know who *"da Baron"* is (who's squiggled on our wallz) –
graffiti on da bristol streets iz sumtimes total ballz
but Banksy? Well, he's kool, man, c now, modern art iz gud –
its wicked, dude, to spray your wall, not takin down ur hood!

B4 u go, id like to say, i think ur being rude –
if you say textin modern lingo in this way is crude.....
u need to live in newer times, an' *UR* from *'way back, when'* -
you *do* forget, 'snot Roman times, it's *now* two thousand – ten!

ZZZZZZZZZZZZZZZZZZZZZZZZZZZZZZZZZZZZZZZZZZZZZZZZZZZ

F.B. = Facebook

Author's note:- *"You try typing out all that lot on "Word Document" and see how many spell-checker errors and red squiggly lines YOU get!*

Peace, Bro".

"Ireland – her time in rhyme (Part Two)"
Friday August 13th 2010
"An idiot – (ic) guide to the history of............second part",
1540 – 1649

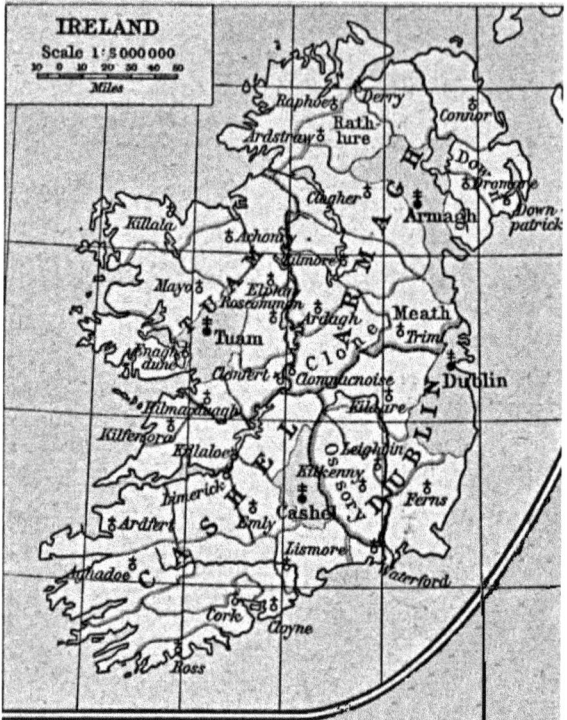

So Henry got his Anne Boleyn
and formed his little church.....
(though, *not* impressed, the Pope –
now Henry's person, he'd besmirch)
But how would he impose his will
upon the Irish clans?
For sure, those stubborn Catholics
had no *"Church of Ireland "* plans!

So thus began a little scheme,
"Plantation", it was called –
he colonised that island
and the natives were appalled!
By *"colonised"*, I'll make it clear
(it made the Irish frown) –
their plots and lands were seized
and handed over to the Crown

And so from English places,
all these colonists did flow –
oh, not forgetting Scotland too,
they ALL wanted to go!
While Catholics were thrown off the land,
the "newbies" settled down –
all in the name of Henry's church,
all loyal to the Crown

Now bit by bit this scheme went on,
it took so many years......
and Henry's *"re-plantation"* scheme
drew many Irish jeers
So all the fertile Catholic lands
were cruelly took away –
all for the *Church of Ireland*,
where the colonists could play!

When Henry died, the English
did go Catholic once again –
and "*Bloody Mary*" did begin
a bloody, violent reign!
But when she died, religion swayed,
a yo-yo for a bit –
"It's Catholic".... *"NO, it's Protestant"*......
"Oh goodness, WHAT is it?"

Now mighty Spain, in worldly terms
was ruler of the globe!
A Catholic country, through and through,
who wore the Papal robe!
Her Navy was all-powerful,
this country ruled the waves –
and so she saw old England
as a bunch of rotten knaves!

"Our nasty rival is a pain,
let's bring the English down!
We'll send a great 'Armada'
now that Lizzie's got the crown!!"
In 1588,
invasion came, and went – and failed!
The good old English spirit –
and the weather too (!) – prevailed......

But Spaniards never gave it up,
they'd try and try again.....
so looked across to Ireland,
thought *"a friend we need to gain.....*
like us, these Irish wear
their Catholic hearts upon their sleeves –
like us, these Irish think
that England's full of rotten thieves!"

"Now if we go to 'Erin's Isle',
our enemy is near....
a handy base, an Irish Sea –
we'll get 'em from the rear!"
And so it came to pass of
an 'Alliance', 'twixt the two –
an Anglo-Irish pact,
to put the English in a stew!

The *'Battle of Kinsale'* took place,
A.D. 1601 –
this little Irish town became
a war-zone, over-run.....
An English force took on the might
of Spain, aligned with *'Eire'* –
now Lizzie's boys had Papal partners
firmly in their stare!

Result of which, it came to be,
the English won a rout!
Which showed the Catholic allies
that she "won't be pushed about!"
Queen Lizzie died, so then we had
King James upon the throne –
who went about reclaiming
bits of Ireland as his own....

In other words, "*Plantation*"
was extended even more -
by 1610, the Ulster bit
saw colonists galore!
These Protestant re-settlers
(each one loyal to King James) –
evicted Catholic counterparts*
despite their* better claims

So what would follow next would be
these "thirty years of hurt" –
evicted Irish Catholics
left to wallow in the dirt....
To say resentment had built up,
is putting rather mild –
result, a ticking time-bomb
and the Irish would go wild!!

By 1641,
old "Charlie First" now had the crown –
and he would get to hear of
a revolt in every town....
cuz' thirty years of pain had spurred
the Irish to rebel –
a tidal wave of violence
for the settlers to repel....

There were babies ripped from wombs
and many houses set on fire,
as the settlers faced the fury
and the wrath of Catholic ire....
So rampaging and looting
thus continued for a time –
King Charlie had a massive job
to overturn this crime......

But then he found more trouble
that was brewing rather near,
now the *Civil War* in England
brought his troubles over here!
So *Cavaliers and Roundheads*, oh –
I'm sure you've heard the tale.....
the upshot of it all was thus –
King Charles was put in jail!

To cut a lengthy story short,
when war was put to bed –
they branded Charlie "traitor"
and decreed he'd lose his head!
So enter Ollie Cromwell,
new *"Protector"* of the land -
claimed England had indulgencies
that needed getting banned.....

But when it came to Ireland,
well, this Cromwell had a plan –
to wipe out every trouble-making
rebel Irish clan....
With this in mind, he took an army –
cutting to the thrust –
he thought "*We need a pest control,
it's slaughter NOW – or bust!*"

TO BE CONTINUED.......

"A doodle door"   **Monday August 16th 2010**

"Visiting a beauty spot in Dorset, after hearing about death-defying plunges into the sea".....

Now if you go to *Durdle Door*,
don't be a dare, just stay a bore –
don't set your ego on the march,
by leaping off that giant arch!

Tomb-stoning off this *"devil's door's"*
a hundred feet up off the floor –
it's best to plan well in advance,
so bring some extra underpants!

"Greetings from Dorset" - (Postcard to a pensioner)
Tuesday August 17th 2010

(But sent as a text instead!)

Oh greetings from the sunny south
(I said I'd write, so shut your mouth!)
The weather's fine and so am I,
I must be quick, time's ticking by.....

The coastline's a Jurassic sort,
on that, not much else to report –
the cliffs all look the same to me,
just stood there, facing out to sea.....

I've sent this message with a pic,
the price of postcards takes the mick!
But Westbay's quite a pretty town,
it's cliffs are coloured yellow-brown

My skin is tinged tomato-red,
it's hurting when I get in bed,
I'll see you when I'm back, old dog,
I must go now, I need the bog.....

"Charmouth Beach"   Wednesday August 18th 2010

"Jurassic coast? That's far too deep – I only want a bit of sleep....."

You won't find peace on Charmouth Beach
the rabble's never out of reach,
wherever wandered, to or fro –
a fossil hunt is on the go!
Along they come with hammers bought
(the item that's most over-sought),
then *BANG-BANG, WHACK-WHACK, DINK-DINK – CHIP!!*
You'll *never* get a decent kip!

"Ode to a Nightingale"
Thursday August 26th 2010

"Mary, Mary.....quite contrary - why don't you smile so?".....

Thou Nightingale! You look so well, when reading out the news!
A shame the stories you relate encapsulate the 'blues'.....
Couldst thou not cheer us up a bit, by reading something fun?
(By that, I *don't* mean *"X Factor"* will grab the Number One!)
Oh Mary, yes I know the drill, it's bad news all the way –
and then a piece towards the end that's kinda light and gay!
If you could say *more* nicer things, sometimes – once in a while –
then maybe we'd observe your face break out into a smile!
I *KNOW* that you're relating stuff you know will bring us down –
but can't you see, as you convey – you do it with a frown?
There *must* be harder jobs around than reading auto-cues –
why is it then you grimace so, when churning out the news?
Or maybe next to Alistair, it's hard to get along –
and you are simply waiting for the 7pm *"bong"*?
If there's a dodgy atmosphere, your viewers will detect –
and when you're babbling on, your moody vibes will thus reflect.....
In future years, you *COULD* become the greatest by a mile –
so grab a newer partner, read some news to make us smile!

"Ode to a *Sky* Lark"   Saturday August 28th 2010

"Mourning the sudden loss of 'Sky Sports News' from Freeview".....

So long, my *"Super Saturday"* – farewell, my three o'clock –
they've took away my '83', that channel's on a block!
I won't hear all the goals go in, NO footer in my room –
no Jeff Stelling to cheer me up, no scores to lift the gloom!
Reporting on the action, with the matches in progress –
was *FREE* on Channel 83, the service did impress.....
Plus all the transfer gossip, round the clock – all day and night –
the *only* sporting service *'Sky'* had offered to the "tight"!
So blast those Murdoch cronies, cuz' they've taken it away!
Why is it, when they get the viewers – *BANG!* You've got to pay!! (??)
Of course, it's *still* available – but I don't have a wish –
to risk my neck upon the roof, by rigging up a dish!
And I'm not funding Murdochs for my weekend footer fun –
I'd rather go without, than pay the owner of *"The Sun"*!

Bye bye, Jeff Stelling – you will be missed!

"Ireland – her time in rhyme (Part Three)"
Sunday August 29th 2010

(1649 – 1690)

In Ireland, Cromwell butchered,
now of that, there is no doubt.....
and he rounded up the ringleaders,
then took the whole lot out!
Drogheda was a place he saw
where there was much ado,
as he slaughtered all the rebels
plus the women, children too......

Now even in these present days,
the name of Cromwell's cursed,
as his place in Irish history
remembers him the worst –
that man, he was a *"Puritan"*,
a butcher, and a knave,
who sent countless Irish citizens
unto an early grave......

One final thought on Ollie
(as his brain did go astray) –
King Charles (in life) closed Parliament
when couldn't get his way –
Now Ollie didn't like this,
so he cursed old Charlie's name –
but when became *"King Oliver"*,
he went and did the same!! (??)

Now moving on, some thirty years
(when Cromwell's in the ground) –
old "Charlie Two" won back the throne,
then next, his brother crowned.....
Now Charlie was a Catholic,
but he'd sought to cover up –
yet on his death-bed, *DID* reveal
he'd drunk the Papal cup

So English folk would get a law,
"No Catholics on the throne" –
though Charlie was a *secret* one,
kid brother James was prone.....
.....to don the papal robes and say
*"the Catholic faith is fine!
You'll never make me give it up,
the choice is solely mine!"*

The Parliamentary powers thought
*"Oh dear, a Catholic King!
I thought we had gone past all that –
a Papal underling!!
Now if we have a 'Roman King',
we're back one hundred years –
old England's back to troubled ways,
a time of little cheers!"*

As "Charlie Two" had left no heir,
('legitimate', at least!) –
in death, in 1685
his crown became released.....
.....To James, who thus became the King
and ruler of the land –
whose Royal reign, our Parliament
would want to see disband!

but –

King Jamie had a daughter,
Princess Mary was her name –
she had *NO* Catholic baggage
and she played no Papal game.....
Now married she, old William,
"Prince of Orange" (of the Dutch) –
in short, she had a little claim
on England's throne, as such.....

So England thought a safer choice
would be a Protestant –
"Queen Mary" and her husband Bill,
a dual throne occupant!
Thought England, *"Yes, we'll have a pair -
snap Jamie's reign in two!"*
(Though Ireland wanted Jamie,
as he was a Catholic too!)

But England knew with Mary,
that they'd have to get a pair –
"Queen Mary" on her own
would seem a trifle bit unfair!
And so it came to be that England
sent an "S.O.S." –
*"Oh 'Royal House of Orange',
come and save us from distress!"*

King Jamie fled to France,
(he was in no mood for a fight!)
And William / Mary *DID* arrive
to claim their Sovereign right!
A *'Glorious Revolution'* it was dubbed
(through lack of blood) –
but "William Three" would have to prove
his reign was not a dud!

Was Jamie going down without
a whimper or a fight?
Or did he claim the English Crown
was his genetic right?

He took himself to Ireland
where he sought his Catholic mates,
then he raised a foreign army
and he checked his diary dates.....

And so the "*Battle of the Boyne*"
took place on Irish lands –
in 1690, Royal fate
did rest in *Erin*'s hands!
King Billy marched an army
and met James beside the Boyne # -
now all that waited, 'fore the fight,
the tossing of the coin!

Now came to be that William
was the victor of the spoils –
the *"Orange"* Protestant
would be the winner of the Royals!
Now Jamie, he returned to France -
'twas never seen again!
The episode in memory, though –
alas, it would remain.....

Now this explains (in present days)
the "*Orange March*" tradition –
July 12th, in Belfast
sees the "winners" on a mission!
To celebrate King Billy
as the victor of the 'Boyne'
(and he even beat old Jamie
on the tossing of the coin!)

Whilst marching is all fine and good,
the *"Orange"* are precise –
to take it down the Catholic street
(provoking isn't nice!)
All dressed in Billy's *"Orange"*,
loudly drumming as they walk(!) –
so rubbing Catholic noses in the dirt,
to make 'em sulk!

It's hated by the Nationalists,
the Catholics too, dislike –
they would have liked to see old William
up and on his bike!
Traditions though, are set in stone -
this march won't go away,
so this little *"Orange"* drumming crew
of course, is here to stay.......

TO BE CONTINUED.....

The River Boyne, County Meath, Ireland

"A Dublin text message" Friday September 3rd 2010

"Genuine message, sent across the Irish capital – I was supposed to be conducting research in the National Library, but........."

"I'm coming to the Library in minute,
in a jiffy –
right now, I'm feeling iffy
cuz' I'm sailing down the Liffey!"

(See – I told you I'm always texting poetry into my phone, *any* time, *any* place.....)

"Life in the money factory"
Monday September 13th 2010

"Confessions of a night-time worker".....

Now *"Mint-X"* is the place to be *
for writing silly poetry –
I think of rhymes when counting cash,
it makes the time go in a flash

I've made the *Bank of England* curse,
cuz' they have seen my little verse –
I think it really gets their goats,
it's written on their ten pound notes!!

See, *how* to make my poems flow,
in busy *"Mint-X"* on the go? *
Cuz' when there's rhyming in my brain,
it's *"write it down"*, or lose again.....

This only leaves one thing to do –
that's "scribble down", (when out of view)
though I've respect, so give me cred –
I *DON'T* write on our Queenie's head!

See, all I get to see is *'beans,'*
when slaving on these drat machines -
your mind is prone to wander, so
I jot down verse, when *'it'* gets slow

If my machine should ever *stop*,
just watch my *'occupation'* swap(!) -
well, *who* can say that it's **my** fault,
when shudders to a grinding halt?

"Excuse me mate, I think you'll find
THIS needs an engineering mind!"
So while he checks the symmetry,
I'm free to write me poetry!

We've got a licence, printing loot,
so, guess I risk the dreaded *'boot'* –
cuz' scribbling much poetic line
puts their p*roduction* in decline!

Yet *who* can say it's such a crime(?) –
it only takes a little time,
tis' just a line, or two (or three) –
and only if my time is free

But now they know, the secret's out –
my manager will scream and shout,
yet if she says *"You've got the sack!"*,
at least I've got my night-times back!

*For security reasons, names of relevant 'Financial Institutions' have been *changed*.

"Lady Molyneaux"
Saturday September 18th 2010

"Ode to a sweet-voiced maiden (Who's well known in Bristol parts)".....

The Upper classes owe a debt
unto the Queen of Etiquette,
known for her sweet tones on the loo –
her name is Lady Molyneaux!

Now can there be a better choice
for title of "Best Singing Voice"?
I've never heard a purer sound –
it's true, I'm not a lying hound!

Her version of *"Our lips are sealed"*
should publically be mass-revealed –
her cover songs of *Girls Aloud*
should not be hidden from the crowd!

Her dulcet tones dance on the ear,
angelic, bliss, so sweet and clear –
it's feels like I'm in heaven when
I hear her, so I say *"Amen!"*

Now ain't somebody got a clock,
I'm sure there must be ONE in stock (?) –
that wakes me up with joyous tunes
by 'Lady Molly' as she croons

I need her songs on my i-Pod,
her talents are a gift from God –
just can't explain my inner joys
on hearing her melodic noise.....

I want her as my ringing tone,
my wake-up call upon my phone –
as long as I'm alive, I'll scream
"Don't take away my vocal dream!"

I never take a day off work,
my job I'll never shun or shirk –
cuz' if I did, I know I'd miss
her tones, so like an angel's kiss.....

You'll never hear me moan or bitch
on hearing her falsetto pitch –
and never shall I groan at things
when Bristol's Shirley Bassey sings

Now when it comes to vocal choice
this 'Lady Moll's' my Rolls and Royce –
she needs to make recording plans,
she is the *Duchess of St Annes!*

Thou maiden, oh your voice so sweet,
I listen and it's such a treat –
and know ye how I've never cussed,
to hear you is a daily must!

I've listened in the *"Horse and Groom"*,
your silky voice lights up the room –
I'd buy your record in the shop,
but promise me, you'll never stop......

"Friday's child" Friday September 24th 2010

"Avoid the Bristol streets at night – you're bound to get a nasty fright....."

Friday's child ain't full of grace,
Saturday's child, kicked in the face –
Sunday's child's an achy head,
Monday's child is stuck in bed......
Tuesday's child is lookin' neat,
Wednesday's child is on the street –
Thursday's child ain't like a monk,
Friday's child is roarin' drunk.....
Saturday's child is lookin' swell,
Sunday's child in is a cell –
Monday's child sat in a park,
Tuesday's child, out after dark.....
Wednesday's child is being sick,
Thursday's child is in the 'Nick –
Friday's child.....

"I'm only here to shop!"
Saturday September 25th 2010

"Unwanted distractions when walking through Broadmead".....

Now if I *must* walk in our town,
I try to keep my noggin down –
pretend I'm on the *dog 'n' bone*,
text utter nonsense in my phone.....

Perhaps make out I'm utter deaf,
I couldn't hear a treble clef –
cuz' this is what you've got to do,
to stop *them* coming up to *you*.....

I am here to shop – so WHY are you following me with a bucket?
I am here to shop – so WHY are you talking about surveys?
I am here to shop – so WHY are you shouting about religion?
I am here to shop – so WHY are you blowing bubbles in my face?

No, I don't want a 'Big Issue' –
No, I don't want to try a sweet –
No, I don't want a "free sample" –
No, I don't want to give you my bank details –

No, I won't pay by monthly instalments.....
No, I'm NOT with the A.A. –
No, I don't WANT to be with the A.A.
Yes, I give to Charity –
*no, not to **your** Charity!*
No, I HAVEN'T got a minute –
(I think you would take five!)

If I had wanted services
provided by A.A. -
then don't you think I would have
sorted out *before* today?
I know your tricks,
you try and catch these people on the hop –
well, don't you dare with *me*, because
I'm only here to shop!

And when I give to charity,
I do it in *MY* time –
I don't just give to *strangers*
in the street, now that's a crime!
I know your game,
you try and pick the meekest of the crop –
well, don't you try and pick on *me*,
I'm only here to shop!

I'll listen to religion
on a Sunday, in a church!
Why should I hear you *now*
and leave my errands in the lurch?
I *know* just what you're shouting,
that "*Society's a flop*" –
well, don't you try and preach to me,
I'm only here to shop!

I see you blowing bubbles in the air,
what's *that* about?
The biggest-ever waste of human time,
without a doubt!
They only last a second,
'fore they end up with a *'pop'!*
Don't wanna burst your bubble, but
I'M ONLY HERE TO SHOP!!!

Now if I stopped for ALL of you,
(five minutes, *every* one) –
I'd lose an hour of my time
and get no shopping done!
So can you wonder, that your "business"
makes me curse and moan?
And *THAT's* why I pretend
I'm talking / texting in my phone!

GO AWAY!!   *I AM ONLY HERE TO* **SHOP*!!*

"A letter to my leader"
Sunday September 26th 2010

"Posted to Ed Miliband, on hearing news of his election to be the new leader of the Labour Party".....

Dear Edward,

Although your brother Dave was seen
the one most fit to lead –
it seems the 'nod' has gone to you,
the youngest of the breed
I made my choice in all good faith,
your brother got my vote –
but now you've pipped your Elder,
well, that man has missed the boat....

Of all the other candidates,
there weren't too many calls -
demanding Mr Burnham's name,
or that of Mr Balls.....
and Diane – NEVER credible
as future Labour voice -
in other words, at least you were
my easy SECOND choice.....

My disappointment's put aside,
in you I'll follow true –
you'll lead the fight, take on the might
of men that's 'dressed in blue'.....
I hope and pray, with all my heart
you'll challenge all the nuts –
(the leaders of our Government,
who want these Budget cuts!)

At P.M.Q's, you'll stand your ground,
nay, more than that, 'let rip' –
to let that P.M., Davy know,
you're NOT an oily 'pip'!
Because your voice is 'weak and squeak',
you'll have to 'rough the tone' -
much better off, with 'manly gruff',
and NOT your feeble drone.....

When 'Cam' is shouting things at you,
retaliate, annoy –
it's no good simply sitting there,
and sulking like a boy.....
Although he'll dub you 'Boy of Brown',
don't let it hurt you so -
cuz' you know he's the 'Son of Thatch',
now this will land a blow!

I promise you, I'll try my best,
NOT think "What might have been (?) –
if only, Ed, your brother Dave
had won, because......you're 'green'!"
Alas, he'll never serve your team,
there's been a family stink -
farewell, poor Davy – off you go,
the 'back-benches' I think.....

*Congratulations on your win,
I'll offer you my hand —
though grudgingly, (you know I wanted
t'other Miliband!)
But that is in the past, and so
what matters now, the most -
you'll need to grill the government,
turn 'Con Dems' into toast!*

I write to you most faithfully,

your loyal servant..........D. Hurley

"Ireland – her time in rhyme (Part Four)"
Tuesday September 28th 2010

(1700 – 1898)

Eighteenth-Century Ireland saw
the country in a mood,
as decisions made in London
made the Irishmen subdued
This island wanted breaking out
from England's iron fist,
so she had her independence
topping off her shopping list!

"United Irishmen" became
a body to this end,
and it sought to gain self-Governance
for Irish to defend
So Wolfe Tone was a chap who said
"let's try and go alone –
now it's time for a Republic,
so these English MUST be shown!"

Now over many years
this way of thinking gathered pace,
as *"United Irishmen"* began
to clearly put their case.....
So skipping through the decades now
and coming to the boil,
when another great Rebellion
took place on Irish soil....

'twas on the hill of Vinegar *
in year of '98,
it did come to be, the English
cast the rebels to their fate.....
At break of dawn, that day in June
the Irish on the hill –
were boxed in by the English
who then moved in for the kill.....

So yet again, the Irish were
defeated on the field
And the English took away Wolfe Tone,
then saw that he was killed.....
Effectively, this meant that
Irish folk remained as "slaves",
of the ruling British classes
(whom they saw as nasty knaves)

And so an *"Act of Union"*** next,
alas, was put in place,
which saw all the English / Irishmen
unite – a "single race"
At least, that was the *theory*,
though in *practice*, think again,
as Republicans had little thoughts
of serving George's*** reign!

O'Connell**** was an Irishman
who wanted Irish rights
and *Emancipation* # was a scheme
that he had in his sights!
He wanted Catholics free to serve
as MP's if they chose
within England's 'mother Parliament',
along with English foes!

The law you see, had stated
that *NO* Catholics were allowed –
to enter British Parliaments
and mingle with the crowd
But 1847
('twas in the year O'Connell died) –
came disaster, as seen through
Irish farming on the slide.....

The situation was
to make it clear for everyone –
that English landlords ruled the way,
all things under the sun....
The peasant Irish had small plots
of land, in which to tend –
and plant their cheap potatoes
t'which their diets did depend

These snips of land, so tiny,
gave the dwellers little voice –
with farming, mere potato crops
became their *only* choice
By 1846, don't think
this situation eased -
as next, a crop infection
meant the spuds were all diseased....

The Irish had a simple choice:-
to eat the rotten spud –
or end up having *nothing*,
lay down starving in the mud.....
Result of which, it came to be,
the country was awash –
of starving people, sickness,
famine, death – and lack of nosh.....

Two million people fled the land,
in ships, they went away
Another million, lucky *NOT* –
they reached their dying day.....
The government of England
had been very slow to act,
so the Irish said *"too little,
and too late – now that's a fact!"*

'Twas yet another reason
for the Irish to complain
they'd been treated by the government
disgustingly again!
As if they needed reason
(which they *DIDN'T*, that's for sure!) -
to push for independence
from the English all the more!

So in the years that followed on
from this catastrophe,
things did come to be of bodies
like the rebel I.R.B. ##
The I.R.B. was founded
with an independence goal –
though it needed to be secret,
so they played a sneaky role.....

This "Brotherhood of Irishmen"
(the I.R.B. for short) –
fore-ran the modern I.R.A,
a "father", of a sort
The movement had a foreign branch,
"The Fenians" – far away.....
(The rebel Irish emigrants,
who'd gone to U.S.A.)

When in a secret "Brotherhood",
it's best to make no sound –
but chip away at British rule
in secret, underground.....
Whilst up above, the politicians
tried to make their case –
and Charlie Parnell ###, new MP,
became the public face.....

In Britain, leaders came and went,
yet still, the issue burned.....
could Irish folk be trusted
with their independence earned?
The Liberal William Gladstone came
and he foresaw events –
deep down, he *knew* an "Irish Bill" ####
long-term, made common sense.....

With Irish feelings running high,
he guessed they'd *not* relent –
the *very least* they wanted was
self-ruling Government
Now, several tries – "One", "Two" *and* "Three",
he introduced a Bill –
yet *every* time, they'd vote it down,
against old Willie's will......

For all he tried, alas, old Parnell,
he came crashing down –
when took a mistress, got found out,
it made him look a clown!
So *"Home Rule"* Bills, one, two and three
were *NEVER* passed at all –
which made it feel like Irish heads
were banging a brick wall!

While Englishmen were passing laws,
(extension of the vote) –
it seemed the Irish saw no gain,
which really got their goat!
In '98, old Gladstone's life
was ended - passed away.....
a *"Home Rule"* Bill, or so it seemed,
would *not* see light of day.....

TO BE CONTINUED.....

* Battle of Vinegar Hill, County Wexford, 1798
** 'Act of Union' (1801), unifying the Kingdom of Great Britain with the Kingdom of Ireland
*** King George III, King of England from 1760 to 1820
**** Daniel O'Connell, *"The Liberator"*, 1775-1847
\# Catholic Emancipation = greater freedom for Catholics, including the right to sit in the Houses of Parliament
\#\# I.R.B. = Irish Republican Brotherhood
\#\#\# Charles Stewart Parnell (1846-1891), who became the *'Home Rule League'* MP for County Meath in 1875.
\#\#\#\# Irish 'Home Rule Bill'

"Three cheers for Mr Archibald"
Thursday September 30th 2010

"Of Bristol folk, now here's a 'peach' – it's Mr Grant.....or is it Leach?".....

Three cheers for Mr Archibald!
- and movie stars like he!
Oh pardon me, it's *"Cary Grant?"*
His name escapeth me!
Whichever tag you know him by,
I think it's fair to say –
he *was* the greatest movie star
who acted in his day!

Hooray for Mr Cary Grant!
- the actor, oh so fine!
Who really knew the art of
giving out that killer line.....
I praise up *"His Girl Friday"*
and I love *"North by Northwest"* –
the movies made with Hitchcock
were amongst his very best!

A normal Bristol lad at heart,
he went to U.S.A. –
to see if there were vacancies
in film – with decent pay!
But when you come from *Brizzle*,
well, you don't expect a job –
like "Leading man in Hollywood"
and Number One heart-throb!

Now when I'm down the *Odeon*,
I think *"Hallo there, Leach!*
How Hollywood has changed today,
you'd have so much to teach!
I guess that in the pecking order,
you'd still be above -
the likes of Pitt and Clooney,
yes, you'd still be called 'The Guv'!"

So when I'm up in Horfield
(no, it's *NOT* to see *'The Gas'*) -
I often pass his house, and muse
"this Leach was different class!"
Though Cary was a wanderer,
wherever he would roam –
he'd *always* come to Bristol,
cuz' he knew it was his home.....

When poor old Cary passed away,
in 1986 –
we Bristol folk declared he was
the greatest man in "flix".....
Let's ring his praises out again,
in book, and song, and speech -
and make sure we ain't heard the last
of good old Archie Leach!

"Ode to the Robin" Saturday October 2nd 2010

"One for the Bristol City.....Two for the boys in red....
Three for the chaps down College Green, we'll badger till we're dead!"
(Football and politics in Bristol)

Thou Robin! I enjoy your song,
(when you *"come bob – bob – bob along"*),
and flying over Ashton Vale,
see country from a different scale -
you dream of viewing stadiums
that's fit for new Millenniums.....
so chirping out, you sing your verse
(though Mr Lansdown holds the purse):-

"Wake up, wake up – you sleepyheads,
get up, get up – get out your beds –
we want a newer pitch re-laid,
so better football can be played –
if Bristol City thus competes,
they'll need these 30,000 seats!
Oh Council, can't you hear my plea?
We need to do this properly!"

Oh Robin, yes I *do* agree,
I've watched you fly south-westerly –
and noted how you've swooped and spied
those fields next to the *'Park and Ride"*
I'm hoping that good sense prevails,
that *'Sainsburys'* won't go off the rails –
so fingers crossed, they'll take the bait,
which *is* the land at Ashton Gate!

"Scrumpy" the Robin

"Ode to our beautiful river"
Thursday October 7th 2010

"I see the Avon flowing with much mud!".....

Oh Avon! I admire your waters, deep and chocolate brown!
And how you flow majestically, through our majestic town!
Although your summer stench attracts a thousand Bristol moans –
"May God bless all who float on you!" - (three dozen traffic cones!)
So many happy boyhood days were spent on watching you –
your rising tide sub-merging *Asda* trolleys in you too!
I know it's been a little while since I sat on your bank –
but last time that I tried it, I'm afraid my bottom sank!
Oh Avon, how it warms my heart to think of glories past -
(the *"Britain"* floating down you, and she didn't need a mast!)
Now Brunel's bridge looks over you, from town to "Horse-Shoe Bend" –
a pleasant sight? Not on your Nell', I wish I could pretend!

"Tart FM"   **Saturday October 9th 2010**

"The trouble with a certain local radio station....."

There's no room in my Heart for 'Tart'

"More musical variety"?? You're kidding, right – a laugh?
REPEATING things like *that*, you've got more neck than a giraffe!!
Your claim of keeping playlists fresh, this really is a myth!
So for a *start*, for god's sake *'Tart'* – STOP PLAYING AEROSMITH!!
"I do not want to miss a thing" – over, over again!
Just change the disc and start anew, it's driving me *insane!!*
"I heard it through the grapevine" – oh, surprise – we know that s**te.....
methinks I suffer *déjà – vu,* you **didn't** play last night??

oooo, *"Dirty Dancing"* – *"Hungry Eyes"*- et al - *""She's like the wind"* –
I think you've worn these CD's out, time surely they were binned?!
Ah, Mr Bedingfield *AGAIN*, it seems we're out of luck –
now is it *not* the case that *'Tart'* has got it's needle stuck?!
Oh, Luther Van' – (God rest his soul) – I've *nothing* 'gainst this chap –
but as for *"Dancing with his pa"*, this surely needs a nap?!
Take That! How *'Tart'* must follow these, wherever they may roam –
they're playing all their bloody songs, until the cows come 'ome!

The records are *repeats!*
The jingles are *repeats!*
The adverts are *repeats!*
EVERYTHING – *repeats!*

"More musical variety"!! - the logo, come what may........
REPEATED on this station, mere *two hundred* times a day!
A *contradiction,* don't you think? *Hypocrisy* as well!
Now under *'Trade Description Act',* you'd find yourselves in jail!
Oh how I curse the night-shift, where the workers tolerate
all these over-echoed themes of *'Tart'* - repeating on a plate!
Yet how they seem to lap it up, like piggies at a trough -
*"please, try another frequency - and turn that station **off!!**"*

GO AWAY!!   **CHANGE THE RECORD!!**

Concise Oxford Dictionary
Variety – *"being various, diversity, absence of monotony or uniformity, many sidedness"*

Encarta World English Dictionary
Variety –*"the quality of being varied or diversified, a collection of varied things"*

"The Ten Commandments"
Sunday October 10th 2010

"A poetical re-working of words from the Good book."

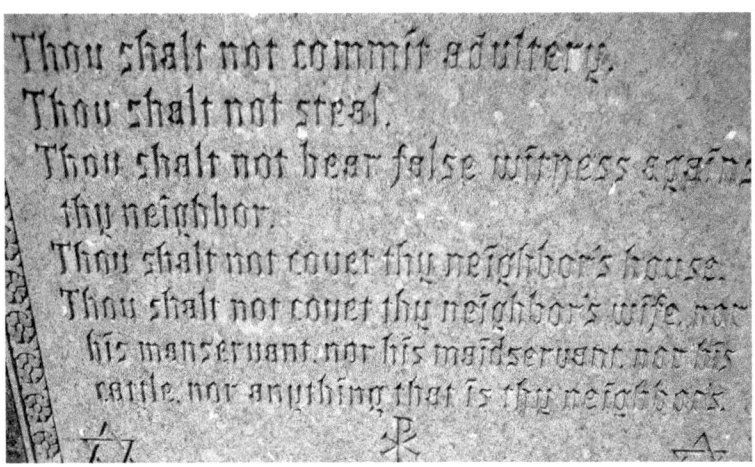

1. There are no *other* gods - except myself,
   now can't you see?
   So if you worship *anyone*,
   'make sure it's only me'

2. You know how I'm a jealous god,
   don't follow 'fakers', please –
   concerning all these 'idols',
   'well, you shouldn't worship these'

3. Dirty words, bad language, swearing,
   leaves a nasty stain -
   I hope you *won't* mis-use my name,
   'nor shout it out in vain'

4. Now after six days slog and toil,
   your Sabbath should be free –
   therefore I think it's fair you keep
   'your Sundays just for me'

5. Your parents have created you,
   behave, don't make 'em mad –
   let's put it in another way,
   'respect your mum and dad'

6. Of all the sins, to *murder*,
   well, the thought gives me a chill –
   I shouldn't have to tell you this,
   'I don't want you to kill"

7. Now once you're wed, don't hop in bed
   with *any* cheatin' hound -
   or put in nice and simple terms,
   'you shouldn't play around'

8. Now things which don't belong to you,
   don't snatch, or hook, or reel.....
   in other words, I'm telling you –
   'I don't want you to steal'

9. For people who's next door to you,
   don't slander, spin a lie –
   I'd rather you were neighbourly,
   'don't hang 'em out to dry!'

10. You shouldn't want your neighbour's wife,
    his ox, his watch and rings.....
    so basically, I'm telling you,
    'don't covet all his things'

Note:-

In 1536, the *powers-that-be* condemned William Tyndale to death, on a charge of '*Heresy*'.
His crime? He wanted to bring the words of the Bible to the common man, by daring to translate it into *"Common English"* so that *everyone* could read and understand it for themselves, without the need of a Priest reciting away in latin.
Yet that was NOT '*Heresy*', and in this day and age when many British children have barely heard of a Bible and know very little of it's contents - neither is *this*.

"Ireland – her time in rhyme (Part Five)"
Monday October 11th 2010

(1900 – 1922)

Michael Collins (1890-1922)

Re-capping now, (cuz' this might prove
quite handy in a bit) –
of how things stood in 1900,
'fore the fuse was lit.....
See, Irish feelings differed
in the North, than from the south –
and *other* things were coming
from the native Ulster mouth

The Protestant majority,
("descendants" of the Kings –
the ones who were "re-planted"
as King Henry's underlings) –
these people in the Ulster north
quite liked the *status-quo* -
they had NO Independence dreams
and didn't want to "go"!

Compare that to the "southerners"
who *DIDN'T* like the Crown –
instead they strove to free themselves
and bring the English down!
They needed newer bodies
which would thus intimidate -
they wanted a *Republic* NOW
and weren't prepared to wait.....

"*Sein Fein*" (it means *'Ourselves alone'*)
was formed in Nineteen-Five,
with it's stated aim to keep
the Independence dream alive
A man named Arthur Griffith
was the brains behind the plan –
which strove to strike the fear of God
in every Englishman!

"*Sinn Fein*" would gain an "army wing"
to give it extra clout -
with fully trained-up terrorists
and bombs to chuck about.....
And from the south, Mick Collins
was attracted to the cause –
in years to come, the English
would perceive him as a nause!

But three years 'fore the I.R.A. #
there came historic scenes,
when the rebels stormed the G.P.O. ##
(which blew to smithereens)
There declaring a "Republic"
(though it was a dodgy claim),
then the ringleaders were rounded up –
or perished by the flame.....

The "Declaration" plan had failed,
though violence wouldn't cease –
for years, these games of "cat and mouse"
they daily, would increase....
The British sent the *"Black n Tans"*,
a vicious army gang –
to counter-act the I.R.A.
and break it with a bang

The I.R.A. refused to go
(intelligence was good) –
this Collins, to the English,
he became like Robin Hood!
The terror of the *"Black n Tans"*
he always seemed to know -
the whereabouts of English,
all the places they would go!

So cloak and dagger, cat and mouse,
relentless, on it went.....
guerrilla warfare, ambushes –
an everyday event....
One morn' in 1920
saw a British spy-ring shot -
the I.R.A. was blamed at once,
which spawned another plot.....

That afternoon in Croke Park
came a Gaelic football match –
the *"Black n Tans"* would get revenge
upon that Dublin patch.....
they opened fire, on the crowd,
and even on the field –
an awful day in history,
when fourteen men were killed.....

Now clearly, this could not go on
and something had to give,
as these daily acts of violence
were NOT a way to live.....
Lloyd-George* believed the time had come
to cut the Irish loose –
he knew they had – (for far too long) -
been strangled by the noose

In '21, the Irish leaders
came to London town –
to talk about how *Eire* could be
relinquished from the Crown
Mick Collins (though against his will)
was chosen on the team,
and along with Arthur Griffith –
they would push the Irish dream

The Treaty plan decided on
resulted in a *split* –
with Ireland's Kingdom cut in two
("The South" and *"Ulster"* bit)
The Protestant majority,
the British would *retain* –
or *Ulster* ("Northern Ireland" –
that's the name it would obtain)

Now Collins signed the document,
so Irish folk might claim -
the *Treaty* was a botch-up job,
and HE had been to blame!
The country being split in two,
left Ulster "cast away" –
(that's kept within the British Isles,
and not allowed to stray)

The "southerners" had dreamt
the WHOLE of Ireland would be free –
they hadn't banked on Ulster
staying British property!
Had Collins been a "traitor"
to the Independence cause?
And when he signed the Treaty
did he ever stop and pause?

The *"War of Independence"*,
in effect, it fizzled out –
but in it's place, more sinister,
an outcry came about.....
When came down to the *Treaty*,
there were feelings running deep –
and whether you were *"FOR"* or not,
the road to peace was steep.....

So years of fighting English
in the name of *"Eire alone"* -
then when they'd half-attained it,
they would fight amongst their *own*.....
The Irish *"anti-Treatyists"*
thought Collins caused the strife –
in short, he had a struggle on
to keep his very life.....

In '22, at *Béal na mBláth*
they shot Mick Collins down –
a travesty, that man had severed
Ireland from the Crown
The country went in mourning,
as the War, it died away –
the *Irish Free State* had arrived,
it's still around today.....

TO BE CONTINUED......

POBLACHT NA H EIREANN.
THE PROVISIONAL GOVERNMENT
OF THE
IRISH REPUBLIC
TO THE PEOPLE OF IRELAND.

IRISHMEN AND IRISHWOMEN In the name of God and of the dead generations from which she receives her old tradition of nationhood, Ireland, through us, summons her children to her flag and strikes for her freedom.

Having organised and trained her manhood through her secret revolutionary organisation, the Irish Republican Brotherhood, and through her open military organisations, the Irish Volunteers and the Irish Citizen Army, having patiently perfected her discipline, having resolutely waited for the right moment to reveal itself, she now seizes that moment, and, supported by her exiled children in America and by gallant allies in Europe, but relying on her own strength, she strikes in full confidence of victory.

We declare the right of the people of Ireland to the ownership of Ireland, and to the unfettered control of Irish destinies, to be sovereign and indefeasible. The long usurpation of that right by a foreign people and government has not extinguished the right, nor can it ever be extinguished except by the destruction of the Irish people. In every generation the Irish people have asserted their right to national freedom and sovereignty; six times during the past three hundred years they have asserted it in arms. Standing on that fundamental right and again asserting it in arms in the face of the world, we hereby proclaim the Irish Republic as a Sovereign Independent State, and we pledge our lives and the lives of our comrades-in-arms to the cause of its freedom, of its welfare, and of its exaltation among the nations.

The Irish Republic is entitled to, and hereby claims, the allegiance of every Irishman and Irishwoman. The Republic guarantees religious and civil liberty, equal rights and equal opportunities to all its citizens, and declares its resolve to pursue the happiness and prosperity of the whole nation and of all its parts, cherishing all the children of the nation equally, and oblivious of the differences carefully fostered by an alien government, which have divided a minority from the majority in the past.

Until our arms have brought the opportune moment for the establishment of a permanent National Government, representative of the whole people of Ireland and elected by the suffrages of all her men and women, the Provisional Government, hereby constituted, will administer the civil and military affairs of the Republic in trust for the people.

We place the cause of the Irish Republic under the protection of the Most High God, Whose blessing we invoke upon our arms, and we pray that no one who serves that cause will dishonour it by cowardice, inhumanity, or rapine. In this supreme hour the Irish nation must, by its valour and discipline and by the readiness of its children to sacrifice themselves for the common good, prove itself worthy of the august destiny to which it is called.

Signed on Behalf of the Provisional Government,
THOMAS J. CLARKE.
SEAN Mac DIARMADA. THOMAS MacDONAGH,
P. H. PEARSE. EAMONN CEANNT.
JAMES CONNOLLY. JOSEPH PLUNKETT.

The I.R.A. was formed in 1919

"The Easter Rising", 1916, when Irish Nationalists seized the General Post Office in Dublin and proclaimed a declaration of Independence for Ireland

* David Lloyd George, Prime Minister of the United Kingdom between 1916 and 1922

"Let's throw an egg at Mr Clegg"
Wednesday October 13th 2010

"Enough said....."

"Let's throw an egg..........at Mr Clegg –

or kick him hard.............upon his leg –

to take him down........ a peg!!" *(or two)*

Um. That's it.....

"4:25pm (A dream)"
Wednesday October 20th 2010

*"This afternoon, 4:25pm, found myself awaking from a nightmare – only to find that some of it was **true**. Because at the core of every dream, there lies more than a hint of reason and reality....."*

The clock showed *four and twenty-five*,
when London dreamt itself alive.....
those blackened clouds......an ugly frown,
high over this unhappy town.....

A "ghost-ship", one of Bristol's gems.....
"The Matthew", surging down the Thames –
headlong, towards the strangest sight,
of *'Clifton Bridge'*, in all it's might.....

Onboard, their plans had been delayed -
(*Petition*, and a Mass Parade),
it's too late now, they could have stayed,
the *Big* decisions *have been made*.....

Through all these months, they've *talked the talk*,
but now it's time to *walk the walk*.....
for England's nightmare's come alive –
the clock shows *four and twenty-five*.....

C.S.R. 20/10/10 #

"Poem for the Polish / Poemat dla Polakow"
Friday October 22nd 2010

"A trochę bezczelny bardzo, ale to ja jestem tylko stara się być przyjazny....."

Polska!

Zapraszamy was z otwartymi ramionami,
Wiec witajcie na Naszym brzegu!
Czujcie swobodę przychodząc i odchodząc,
Teraz gdy nasze drzwi już nie są przeszkodą!

Widzimy Was radzących sobie,
Z niegrzecznością Nam nie po drodze –
gazety Wasze drukując,
jak i jedzenie przechowując!

Kwalifikacja Wasza jest zbyt wielka
na oferowanych prac miejsca –
ale podatki placicie szczerze,
co wygadanych ust naszych strzeże!

Marie Curie Waszą lubimy
Melodii Chopina nie pogardzimy -
będziemy chwalić Kopernika Waszego,
żaden dla Nas blazen z Polańskiego!

O to nadzieja, ze będziecie rozkwitać,
Nowych przyjaciół wciąż witać –
Wielkiej Brytanii doświadczenia życiowe
powinny w dywidendach być odplacone!

Swietnie!

Note:- Many thanks to Erwin Wozniak for his personal interpretation and subsequent translation from English into Polish. To see the original poem in it's (rhyming) English language format, please turn to Page.....??

"Three cheers for Mr Dirac"
Tuesday October 26th 2010

"It's all about Quantum Mechanics, stupid....."

Three cheers for Mr Dirac,
and Equations in his name!
A semi - Swiss Bristolian
who learned the physics game!
His knowledge of *Mechanics* -
(that's the *quantum* ones, of course!) -
would influence technology,
his *brain* was at the source!

Three cheers for good old Dirac,
and the roads named after he!
(I think there's one in Bishopston,
he lived there, 19-3)
The sad thing of his boyhood was,
his father caused a stench –
by forcing poor old Paul to speak
in nothing else but French!

But Dirac was so clever,
he had 'Bristol Uni' plans –
now even Mr Einstein was
amongst his greatest fans!
Progressing onto Cambridge,
(well, you've *got* to make a start!) -
Atomic Theory was the subject
closest to his heart (!)

In 1933, poor Dirac
wanted a disguise –
cuz' he'd become reluctant
to pick up his '*Nobel Prize*'!
See, Paul had been affected
by this shyness since a boy –
(result of dominating tricks
his father would employ).....

Now when I'm walking Park Street,
I do think *"Hallo there, Paul!*
The letters following your name
could fill the Colston Hall!
Your scientific knowledge
has put Bristol on the map –
I'd like to pay you tribute
as a very brainy chap!"

$$g_{rs}, p^{rs} g_{m0} g^{r0}, (-g^{00})^{-1/2} H = \int d^3x [(-g^{00})^{-1/2} H_L - g^{r0}/g^{00} H_r] \ x^0 H_r \ H_L \ H_L \approx 0; \ H_r \approx 0 \ (r=1,2,3)$$

"*The aim of science is to make difficult things understandable in a simpler way; the aim of poetry is to state simple things in an incomprehensible way. The two are incompatible.*" **Paul Dirac.**

"Two Georges"   Saturday October 30th 2010

"Observation poetry, recited with a wink –
we know what Mr Osborne says, so what then does he THINK?"

GEORGE ORWELL (1945) – written in a book called *"Animal Farm"*.....
"All animals are equal – but some are *more* equal than others"

GEORGE OSBORNE (2010) – (apparently) the heir to a multi-million pound wallpaper fortune.....
"We're all in this together....."
(.....but some are *more* 'in it' than others.....)??

Or put another way -

George One:–
"All animals are equal,
that I'm proud to say, my brothers.....
yet some of them, regret to say –
are *MORE* equal than others!"

George Two:-
"We're all in this together,
as the Coalition smothers.....
yet some of us, it's true to say –
are 'in it' *MORE* than others!"

"The Guy Fawkes Dilemma (1605)"
Friday November 5th 2010

"What shall we do with him?"

A pony trap for *dragging* him,
a neckerchief for *gagging* him –
carriage-wheels for *grinding* him,
red-hot pokers *blinding* him –
cable cords for *strangling* him,
and secondly, for *dangling* him –
a kitchen knife for *shaving* him,
the carving knife *engraving* him –
(in other words, for *cutting* him,
then afterwards, *de-gutting* him)-
a vat of dye for *casting* him,
an angry mob *lambasting* him –

we'll have nobody *guarding* him,
with rotten fruit *bombarding* him –
some needles sharp for *pricking* him,
a builders yard for *bricking* him –
with boulders thrown for *downing* him,
then in the Thames for *drowning* him –
a razor's edge for *cropping* him,
a feller's axe for *chopping* him –
with vices fit for *crushing* him,
in kitchen bowls for *mushing* him –
we're shouting and *berating* him,
and afterwards, *castrating* him –
NO court will be *adjourning* him.....
there will be *NO returning* him.....

suspense will be concerning him.....

.....a bonfire for burning him!

PROCESSION OF A GUY.

"Ireland – her time in rhyme (Part Six)"
Monday November 8th 2010

(1922 – 1972)

 # The penultimate part of this poem actually begins with the moment when the Irish Free State was formally declared, on December 21st 1921

The Irish Free State had arrived
one cold December day # –
and eight months on saw Collins
cruelly taken from the fray.....
His rival, de Valera,
would go on to be P.M. –
(the future Irish would elect
this schemer as their 'Prem')....

In '37, the *Irish Free State*
changed it's name to *"Eire"* –
(the first of several titles ,
'till she found one with some flair!)
In '49, when changed again,
this time it was for good –
"Republic" ## was the chosen tag,
and that's the one which stood

The I.R.A., it always lurked,
and never went away –
they thought the *Treaty* had been flawed,
the thing had gone astray.....
They'd wanted independence, *YES* –
but as a *single* land –
The *Treaty* split the nation up,
(in two)- that wasn't planned!

BUT:-

The Protestant majority
(or Northern Ireland lot) –
they *didn't* like the I.R.A.,
"we're happy, what we've got!
The Catholics have their country now,
they upped and went away –
it doesn't mean we'll go there too –
we're British, come what may!"

The capital of *"Ulster north"*?
It was, of course, Belfast –
but now it would play centre stage
to shadows from the past.....
Religious and political,
there WERE of course, divides –
but *this* is how there came to be
such hatred on both sides:-

The added complication –
there were *other* Ulster guys,
who were members of the I.R.A.,
(retained their Catholic ties).....
In truth, these were minorities,
in Belfast's fair old town –
but this would prove *sectarian*
and wouldn't settle down.....

Though Catholics had their country
(and their independence too) –
their groups who lived in Belfast
weren't *"The Many"*, but *"The Few"!*

Try living in a neighbourhood,
surrounded by these clans –
of overwhelming Protestants,
(NO independence plans!)

Not easy in your daily life -
part of the Catholic few,
when outnumbered by the other faith,
with different points of view!
And don't forget, at "Marching time",
well, things were even worse –
reminding you of what I wrote,
way back, this older verse:-

"Now this explains (in present days)
the "Orange March" tradition –
July 12th, in Belfast
sees the "winners" on a mission!
To celebrate King Billy
as the victor of the 'Boyne'
(and he even beat old Jamie
on the tossing of the coin!)

Whilst marching is all fine and good,
the "Orange" are precise –
to take it down the Catholic street
(provoking isn't nice!)
All dressed in Billy's "Orange",
loudly drumming as they walk(!) –
so rubbing Catholic noses in the dirt,
to make 'em sulk!

It's hated by the Nationalists,
the Catholics too, dislike –
they would have liked to see old William
up and on his bike!
Traditions though, are set in stone -
this march won't go away,
so this little "Orange" drumming crew
of course, is here to stay......."

So, after (near) three hundred years,
this tale was *STILL* re-told –
"King Billy" – *"Battle of the Boyne"*,
re-opened wounds of old.....
All arguments from long ago,
which *SHOULD* have been the past –
instead, re-surfaced once again –
and centred on Belfast!

By 1969,
the Ulster violence would increase –
so London sent the troops in ###
to assist with gaining peace.....
Reaction though, was negative,
the I.R.A. would curse -
they saw the British "meddling"
and they thought it made things worse!

The I.R.A. embarked upon
a merciless campaign –
in years that totalled twenty-five,
they'd leave an ugly stain.....
Now setting bombs in Ulster,
(and in fact, all over *Eire*) –
not minding who they damaged,
cuz' they simply didn't care!

So, fed up with the arguments,
the residents, one day –
they'd hit the Londonderry streets
so they could have their say
Their mission was a peaceful one,
it stood for *civil rights* * –
but TV cameras captured
many catastrophic sights.....

Now British troops were present,
and they panicked, opened fire –
consequences of this action,
clearly, they were dire.....
Resulting in a bloodbath,
it left thirteen people dead -
the *"Bloody Sunday"* massacre
would long live in the head.....

This incident would leave it's mark
on Eire, for many years –
it also put the "building bridges" plan
into arrears
The British armed protagonists
were *NEVER* made to pay –
there's still investigations
that are going on today.....

TO BE CONTINUED.....

"Republic of Ireland" (1949)
The British Army was sent to Ulster (1969) – the start of the 25 year period known generally in Northern Ireland as "The Troubles"
* The Civil Rights march in Londonderry, on "Bloody Sunday"

"There's gonna be a riot!!"
Wednesday November 10th 2010
*(Rudely awoken)..... "Increasing our Tuition fees,
we'll NOT see in fruition, please!!"*

November 2010

Now waking up in bed today, (I'd left the TV on) –
in dreams, I'd heard them chanting of a very nasty con.....
Then, BANG! – I was awake, and just to prove I wasn't mad –
these students, they were singing of the thing which made 'em sad.....

A London Demo was the scene – young people on a walk;
Election manifesto's down the chute was all the talk
The one specific thing, it seemed, that troubled students so –
a broken promise, made by 'Libs' – (that's Mr Clegg and co!)

"Tuition fees" said Mr Nick, *"I pledge to keep them capped"* –
but *that* was back in April, turns out *now*, the plan was scrapped!
These 'Democrats' had done quite well, picked up the 'student vote' –
yet six months on, this change of heart – it really got their goat!

The March became so rowdy and the air, it would turn blue -
the climax came at Millbank, where a riot would ensue.....
But what's the thing which woke me up, the chant that stirred me so?
The student's song of protest that expressed their tale of woe (?):-

*"Nick Clegg..........WHO are you?
You're a Tory too!!"*

*This is the noise that woke me up.
And that is the truth.*

April 2010 – how times have changed for the 'Fib Dems'.....

"Fly the flags – blow the bugles!"
Tuesday November 16th 2010

"Could Willie not afford a ring – the dearest in the land?
He's given poor old Katy one that's bloomin' second-hand!".....

Prince Willie's getting married, *"oh my god, let's have a bash!"*
Oh dear, I've just remembered, now the country's got no cash!
Yet can this handsome bachelor afford this wedded bliss?
With *Con-Dem* coalition cuts, finances gone amiss?

Last week did see the London streets awash with student cries –
but *WHO* paid Wills' tuition fees? (Were surely quite a size!)
Our Prince's safety's guaranteed, that's with NO "Ifs" or "Buts" (?) –
compared to *OUR* protection with these mass policing cuts?

And is he on the *waiting list* whenever he gets ill?
You what? He never queues in line? Which blighter pays the bill?
Has Willie Windsor got a job, and worried of the dole?
And does he pay his *Council Tax* within his royal role?

Did Willie bail the bankers out, with tax-payers like *us*?
And does he pay *'Congestion Charge'* - perhaps he goes by bus?
Now *why* do politicians think this news will cheer us up?
In current times, we're hardly drinking from the *'Royal cup'*!

"Fantastic news!" says Cameron, a break from 'cutting' rows –
some joy at last for Britain, through exchanging wedding vows!
But we are far too busy being *"All in it together"* –
the country has no money and we're all under the weather!

It's just like back in '81, these *'Cons'* want 'Brownie marks' –
remember poor Diana, and her 'summer wedding' larks?
*Con*spiracies, *Con*spiracies – I'll think I'll shut my gob –
before I face the wrath and fury of the 'Upper mob'!

But one last thing – oh, what surprise! More news to make me ill -
Policing and Security? It's *US* who'll foot the bill!
**When Willie is 'King Billy' and old Charlie's gone away –
will Britain still be in the mess that's facing it today?**

AFTERTHOUGHT:- "Stuff your Bank Holiday – I'll not take it!"

"Scandal Days" Saturday November 20th 2010

"The grabbing hands grab all they can, all for themselves.....after all, it's a competitive world - everything counts in large amounts"......
(M.L.Gore – Depeche Mode)

Electric's going up.....

Gas is going up.....

Water's going up......

Insurance premiums, going up.....

Cost of living's going up.....

V.A.T.'s going up.....

Petrol's going up.....

Beer's going up.....

Bus fares going up.....

Council Tax – up.....

I've got a tax bill for £500 -

The Inland Revenue wants our money.....

"But take our quiz – text us now to win a prize"

GMTV wants our money.....

"Lorraine" wants our money.....

"Loose Women" want our money.....

"I'm a Celebrity" wants our money.....

"X Factor" wants our money.....

"Strictly" wants our money

"Children in Need" wants our money.....

The BBC wants our money.....

Vodafone wants our money.....

Orange wants our money.....

EVERYONE wants our money –

EVERYTHING goes up......

nothing comes down -

Except:-

Police numbers going down .....

hospital staff going down.....

teachers going down.....

Benefits going down.....

Heads going down.....

Morale's going down.....

The country's going down.....

Yet they want us buying cars.....

They want us buying Wii's.....

They want us buying Blackberries.....

They want us buying i-phones.....

They want us buying i-tunes.....

They want us buying i-pods.....

They want us buying i-pads.....

They want us buying holidays.....

Christmas.....

Valentines.....

Easter......

Mothers.....

Fathers.....

Summer......

Holidays......

Halloween.....

Fireworks......

Christmas......

The shops want our custom.....

The gym wants our custom.....

The Movies - our custom.....

the Multiplex......

McDonalds.....

Burger King.....

Argos.....

Next.....

wants our custom.....

Charity wants our money.....

People with buckets.....in town – want our money.....

Internet hackers.....(our details!) – want our money.....

The Council – for parking our cars – want our money.....

The Council – for parking on lines – want our money.....

The Council – for driving in town – want our money.....

The Council – for driving too fast – want our money.....

The shops want our money.....

The banks want our money.....

"Accounts overdrawn (?) – NOT allowed – want our money!

Electric's in profit, by the billion – yet again.....

The Gas's in profit, by the billion – yet again.....

The Water's in profit, by the billion – yet again.....

The Bankers in profit, by the billion – yet again.....

There's not enough money for Rooney to play –

so pay him his due, he's refusing to stay.....

and Cowell is laughing away at the Bank –

the Nation's to blame, we're as thick as a plank.....

See, despite the winter weather,

well, *"We're all in it together"* -

And Cheryl wants our custom.....

and Simon wants our custom.....

and Brucie wants our custom.....

Celebrity -*"OK"* -*"Hello"*-

want our custom!

And "Give us your money for *'Children in Need'*,

the celebrities beg us (purveyors of greed)

Yet still:-

Electric wants paying.....

Gas wants paying.....

Water wants paying.....

Insurance wants paying.....

Tanks want filling.....

The council wants paying......

The Taxman wants paying.....

"Lorraine" wants her cut.....

Simon – his cut.....

"Strictly" – their cut.....

The shops want their cut.....

the movies, their cut.....

McDonalds, their cut.....

Argos, their cut.....

Charity, their cut.....

THERE IS NO MONEY LEFT.....

we have *nothing* more to give.....

Watch the rich getting fatter -

the poor getting thinner -

These are wretched days.....

it's an evil phase.....

they are vile ways.....

These are Scandal days.....

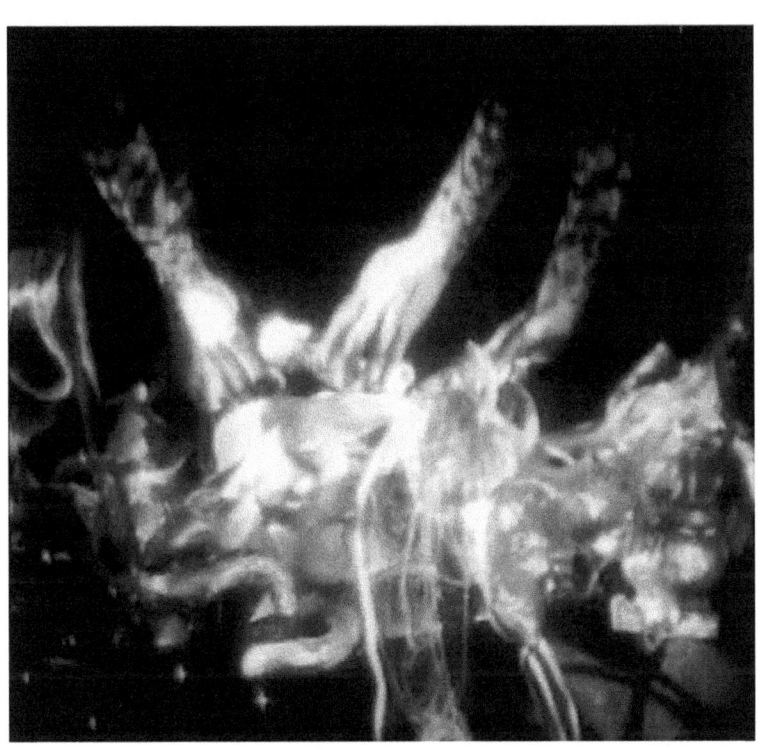

"Man's pest friend" Monday November 22nd 2010

"Continuing troubles between me and the dog".....

Holly, put the kettle on,
let's have a cup of tea –
it's quiet now, there's no-one here,
it's only you and me.....

Holly, stop your whining girl,
I've really had enough –
been up all night,
a headache's got me feeling rather rough!

Holly, why you barking now?
There's *NO-ONE* at the door!
The post is through the letterbox
and now it's on the floor.....

Holly, do you really think
you're getting more to eat?
You've finished off your bacon,
now there is NO other treat!

Holly, yes you know
the chocolate drops are in that drawer –
I'm telling you, you've had *enough*,
you *WON'T* get any more!

Holly, no more tickles girl,
I really must decline –
be off and find your bed because
I'm getting into mine.....

"Five have an awfully spiffing time"
Sunday December 5th 2010

"or 'Five go off to Doncaster'......or 'Five in the 'orrible north'......or 'Five get stuck in a mineshaft'.......or anything else you want it to be called".....

| Biffer | Pongo | Ann | George | Ginger "Lib" the dog |

Stave One

"It seemed so many summers ago now that Biffer and Pongo had been on that wonderful school-holiday adventure together – finding buried treasure at Bullingdons' Creek whilst ship-wrecked on Eton Island. But that was all a long time ago now – what really mattered was that the "Fabulous Five" were all together again! Excitedly anticipating what wonderful new adventures or mysteries were awaiting them next, as they prepared for their latest holiday escapade – a caravan break in a small field just outside Doncaster. In the bleak north........Doncaster! A place that none of the 'Five' had ever heard of before! But it was destined to be a place that they would never forget"........

Now Biffer was the eldest one,
so handsome, tall and blonde –
and Pongo was the second one,
whom Biffer held so fond.....

Then Ann – so meek and lady-like,
the "mother" of the clan –
who organized the picnics
so they always went to plan.....

And cousin George was next in line,
who longed to be a boy –
to look after financial things
for all the *"hoi polloi"!*

Then Ginger "Lib" (the dog), had been
adopted as a pet.....
.....by Georgy 'boy', (to whom he owed
this very special debt)

(Now George had fell in love when
he had first met Ginger *"Lib"* -
this pooch was from the *other* side of town,
and that's no fib!)

So off they set for Doncaster,
(or fields outside the town) –
a lengthy journey, way *"oop North"* -
the prospect made 'em frown!

But with this trek, they'd punctuate
with stops that would include:-
the chance to rest, recuperate,
and buy some smashing food!

Now Georgy held the purse strings,
thus controlling money-flow –
so when it came to shopping,
they were careful with the dough!

And *"Tesco's"* was invaded
by four children and a hound –
selecting food was so much fun,
a spiffing trip all round!

A caravanning holiday!
It really felt so grand!
As far away as Doncaster -
a northern spot.....so bland!

The group of course, had come by bike –
with Ginger in a box –
(pursued by limousines, which brought
their food and clothing stocks!)

Now when the clock said "tea-time"
on their first night in the 'van' –
well, what a feast awaited them,
prepared of course, by Ann!

Smoked salmon in the sandwiches,
and cucumber and ham!
Caviar, rice pudding, fruit –
and double pots of jam!

Champagne all round for everyone!
(for Ginger, ginger beer!) –
oh, what a meal for one and all,
it raised a jolly cheer!

"Oh golly, Ann - you marvel!"
uttered Biffer, looking smug –
then pleased as punch, leaned over,
giving blushing Ann a hug!

"Oh Biffer, don't be silly –
how you spoil and pamper me!
Don't want to see you starving,
I'm just being motherly!"

"Nonsense Ann – you are a whizz!"
said Pongo, with a smile –
"Of all the cooks in all the world,
you're greatest by a mile!"

"Woof!" came Ginger's comment,
(having eaten all the crumbs) –
he *knew* that Ann had tasty ways
of filling up their tums!

"Three cheers for darling Annie!!"
(cousin George proposed a toast) –
"HIP HIP HIP HIP!" – (you *know* the rest,
I'm giving up the ghost!)

But when it came to bed-time,
well, the *"Five"* could settle down –
agreed on how exciting it was,
sleeping out of town!

As usual, Ginger spent the night
curled up round George's feet –
with one ear cocked, in case of
night-intruders from "the street!"

But Georgy slept uneasy,
sensing all was *not* okay –
for horrid people lived nearby,
he wanted them at bay!

Cuz' *"Nasty Edward"* was a well-known
jumped-up little brat –
whom George perceived as no more
than a common dirty *rat*!

"Nasty Ed".....

They *all* knew *"Nasty Edward"* (Miliband)
had wicked aunts –
including *one* who took a really
horrid little stance.....

See, wicked Aunty Harriet
was known for loathing dogs –
believing they were dirty things
who dropped too many *'logs'*.....

But most of all, this wicked aunt -
she hated *'Ginger'* hounds –
believing they made far too many
wretched barking sounds.....

How rotten it made Georgy feel
while knowing nasty aunts –
would curse his darling Ginger's name
within her evil rants!

"Wicked Aunty Harriet".....

The *'Five'* were early risers
in the morning, for the farm –
but walking to the nearest one
(for eggs) – they found alarm!

For *who* should they find resident (?) -
one certain *"Nasty Ed"*!
Not only him – his wicked aunt!
(Though she was still in bed).....

Receiving eggs from Edward,
did see Georgy in a mood –
and likewise, Ginger's head was down,
though never meant it rude.....

Now as the *'Five'* were leaving
well, they *did* get quite a shock -
as "*Nasty Edward*" stood in front of George,
and tried to block!

(Ed):- *"You keep that dog away from me,
and DON'T go near that mine!
If you go snooping there at night,
most likely get a fine!"*

(Biffer):- **"Now won't you steady on, old chap –
there is no need for rants.....
so you be careful I don't knock you
on your underpants!"**

Now walking sullenly away,
the *'Five'* were deep in thought –
and Georgy now was seething
at the eggs that they had bought.....

"Oh Biffer, what's a mine?" said little Ann
(questions galore!)
(Biffer):- **"They're things that Aunty Margaret closed,
in 1984!"**

But "Nasty Edward's" warning –
it had caused their ears to prick –
why *did* this local mineshaft –
and the *'Five'* – get on his wick?

If Aunty Maggie closed it down,
in 1984 –
then what was 'Eddie's' *current* grief?
It bugged them to the core!

Now mightily suspicious, well,
the *'Five'* devised a plan –
involving sneaking round at night
from their old caravan.....

They later worked it out, a scheme,
or, night mine-searching plan –
which would involve, just *three* of them,
that's Pongo, Biff' and Ann.....

Now George's protests were ignored,
they fell on deafened ears –
instead, he was to guard the 'van',
protect their 'break-in' fears!

For "Georgy-porgy", as you know,
he wished to be a boy –
"why couldn't he explore that mine?" -
it really did annoy!

They *knew* that George was safe, of course,
with Ginger at his side –
if any bounders came at night,
they'd get no easy ride!

With night-time drawing in, the 'Five'
were quite beside themselves –
'twas just like all the stuff they'd read
when raiding library shelves!

So off they went with torches,
and away, into the night –
that's Pongo, Biff' and Ann, of course,
no Georgy was in sight!

What danger would the three of them
encounter at the mine?
Could George and Ginger *"Lib"*
protect their fortunes from decline?

Stave Two

"While Biffer, Pongo and Ann were making their way to the mine, George, upset and alone with Ginger, did a shameful thing..........the very thing he hated doing most of all – he cried. He cried and cried and cried until he couldn't cry anymore.....
Why HAD Biffer insisted that he couldn't go to the mine with the others? It was SO unfair!
So George continued crying until he cried himself to sleep.....
In doing so, became unaware of the fact that Ginger had pricked up his ears, and had started growling softly under the blanket.....he didn't hear the growl that had started gently and then picked up to a crescendo.....
Someone was outside - someone was raiding the limousine that had been left by the chauffuer, parked just outside the caravan door.....
And still, George slept........and still Ginger growled......."

Now with a start – *awoken!*
George had left the '*land of nod*' –
and thinking out aloud, exclaimed
"Well, what's afoot? How odd!"

With lack of hesitation,
Georgy leapt straight out of bed -
now made towards the door, with
Ginger *'Lib'* hot on his tread.....

Now leaping from the caravan,
poor Georgy felt perturbed –
as if confirmed, he noticed that
the Limo *was disturbed!*

With doors *akimbo*, boot ajar,
the scene so clear portrayed –
some blighter had concocted
such a wicked night-time raid!

Now in a micro-second,
George could tell what had been *took* –
not only that, this clever boy
identified the crook!

And in a sudden panic
George's heart began to pine -
the *others* were in danger
down that old Doncaster mine??

Put *two and two* together,
(that's the mine-works and the raid) –
now George could sense the *others*
could be *stuck*, in need of aid!

So, sprinting from the caravan,
now running for the shaft –
with Ginger at his ankle-side,
that dog, he *wasn't* daft!

But running past the farm in gloom,
alas, yet more alarm.....
a distant figure – spied his course,
now waving out an arm.....

To George's utter horror,
there were lunatics a-loose!
'Twas wicked Aunty Harriet,
now screaming out abuse!

"We told you – don't go near that mi –
'ere, what's that rusty thing?
You're taking ginger rodents
on your midnight rambling??"

But Georgy-boy, though full of rage,
continued on his way –
and Ginger too, ignored the jibes
no time for such delay!

Arriving at the mine-shaft,
George's mind became a blur –
which way to turn? Now how he wished
the *'Five'* could thus confer.....

Yet stumbling in the dark,
he found a *hole* – a downward climb.....
descending thus, with little fuss,
to see him – oh, sub-lime!

See clever George had brought a rope,
down which, he slowly crept –
(with ginger hounds beneath his arm,
that boy was *so* adept!)

Now dropped a massive distance,
George's tootsies found a ledge –
so letting go the rope, he saw
his feet were on the edge!

Then George and Ginger looked about,
near-darkness all around –
three-quarters down the mine-shaft,
yet a quarter from the ground!

Now if this wasn't bad enough,
this place he found himself –
was kind of like a cliff-face,
o'er a chasm, like a shelf.....

Thought George *"Now what a clever boy,*
that I have brought my rope –
just think, if I had come without,
however would I cope?"

But having thought these things, poor George
was startled – by a noise!
'Twas *voices*, not too far away,
yes, *Ann* – and t'other boys!

"Oh Pongo! Biffer! Darling Ann!
Thank god you're safe and sound!
Now what a queer and horrid place
this is, here underground!"

Said Pongo – *"George, you marvel!*
Oh my stars, we're glad you're here!
Cuz' we've got stuck, our rope was cut,
but now, we're in the clear!"

Then Biffer – *"Spiffing show, old fruit,*
well done and all that sort!
Now tell me, what's the crack, old boy –
what things can you report?"

"Oh Biffer boy, I won't be coy,
I bring you wretched news!
Cuz' rotten thieves have come tonight,
and *robbed* us Tory blues!"

"Those bounders stole our **'Thunder'**,
can't you see, it's 'Nasty Ed'?
He's took away our **'Polling lead'**
and shredded all our **'Cred'!"**

"Our **'Moral high-ground'** - stolen, Biff!
Oh goodness, what to do?
That's **'Thunder'**, **'Credit'**,**'Poll-lead'**,
oh my stars, we're in the poo!"

"Those blighters swiped our **'Ethics'**,
and our '**moral right to lead**'-
so, thanks to *"Nasty Edward"*,
we've become *Children in Need* !"

"They've taken **'Popularity'**,
it's stolen, 'twas a breeze!
(That Mr Clegg! I curse his name!
- and *that* of 'Student Fees!!)"

"Those *eighteen* years it's taken us
to find these treasured things –
yet six months on, they've gone *again*,
now plucking *Labour* strings!"

"Oh, can't you see? What *can* we do?
They're stolen, gone amiss!
Let's elevate! Evacuate!
Get *out* of this abyss!"

But *who* did they find looking down,
from distance, up the shaft?
Two little heads, from way up high –
this mine was *over-staffed*!

Yes – *Edward!*..... and his *wicked Aunt!*
Their faces, twisted so.....
contorted, grinning wildly,
now laughing at their woe!

For, to their utter horror,
now the *'Five'* would find it worse –
cuz' Edward, swiftly, silently...........
......a *trick*, to make 'em curse!

Now *out of reach*, poor George's rope,
(for Eddie's hand had grabbed) –
till moving slowly up the hole,
the *'Five'* had been de-fabbed!

So they could only marvel
at this trickery, well crafted –
now true to say, well *this* poor *'Five'*
were well and truly *'shafted'*!

They were *trapped*.......

Said Pongo - "Seems our *'Tory Five'*,
 ain't welcome in this place -
 see, way 'oop north, say, Doncaster –
 they're like a different race!"

Then Ann - *"Oh Pongo, wasting breath!*
 Stop talking utter poo!
 Oh Georgy! Pongo! Biff and Ginge!
 What **are** *we gonna do?...............*"

TO BE CONTINUED – *one* day.........

(Maybe).........

"Cable under the table (A 'fable')"
Thursday November 25th 2010

"Once student-friendly, good old cheese – now, wants to 'up' Tuition Fees".....

"Let's make that Mr Cable..........sit in shame under the table.....

he's proved he isn't 'able'..........and says my Auntie Mabel –

'May even be unstable!'

so stick him with a label..........when he sits under the table".....

"Or lock him in the stable!"

"The road to Weston Pier"
Saturday November 27th 2010

*"Arisen from the ashes, yes, the pride of Weston's back!
I hope you don't mind queuing, cuz' it's under 'Brum' attack!".....*

You won't find local accents on the road to Weston Pier –
in fact, the 'Brummie' dialect's the only one you'll hear!
Why is it that the *'Black Country'* think *"Super-Mud"* is peach?
You would have thought these Midlanders had never seen a beach!
I'm *not* the type of guy who bears a grudge against these chaps
from Birmingham, or Dudley – sundry places on these maps.....
but what's the treat in driving ninety miles in a car,
just for viewing chocolate channels? (that's *IF* you can see that far!!)
There's Brummies on the dodgems, and there's Brummies on the Green –
there's Brummies wanting fish and chips – they're *always* on the scene!
They're walking on the Promenade - they're eating candy floss –
they're *always* finding things to do, and *never* at a loss!
Concerning all these Brummies, well, their holidays are queer –
they're always on the M5, *on the road to Weston Pier.....*

"Ireland – her time in rhyme (Part Seven)"
Sunday November 28th 2010
(1972 – PRESENT)

Now after "*Bloody Sunday*"
well, the I.R.A. got mad -
renewed it's terror campaign
with the bomb – was really bad!
The Massacre had lit the fuse,
it helped the I.R.A.,
now recruiting many members
who signed up without delay.....

So fired with new anger,
setting bombs all over Eire –
and Birmingham, and London –
they were bombing *everywhere!*
The I.R.A. protagonists,
who set things all ablaze –
if they were caught, they'd find themselves
imprisoned in '*The Maze*' *1

By this time, Gerry Adams was
the man who led *Sinn Fein* –
and with his pal McGuinness,
they would prove to be a pain!
This double-act were 'terrorists',
their enemies would claim –
so when there were explosions,
well, this duo got the blame

McGuinness had past terror links,
(this means the I.R.A). –
'twas rumoured too, that Adams*
had – one time – been "in their pay"
The opposition parties reckoned
*HE** was a disgrace –
so Reverend Ian Paisley   *2
wouldn't look him in the face.....

To sum things up (in simple terms),
it's roughly fair to say –
that Gerry Adams and his pal
were viewed with great dismay
The public faces of *Sinn Fein*
(indeed, the I.R.A.) –
two faces that the D.U.P.   *3
would want to go away.....

See, Ian Paisley's D.U.P.
were massively opposed –
to all that *Sinn Fein* stood for,
all the things that they proposed
Now Paisley was a Protestant,
a sort of *'Orange'* man –
and keeping British rule in Ulster
was his major plan.....

So these were the conflicting views   *4
which set the Ulster tone –
the choice to be a *"loyalist"*,
or for *"Ourselves alone"!*
But also, there were splinter groups
and other factions too** –   *5
so many different factors
in this complicated brew!

Returning to the I.R.A.
(their twisted evil schemes –
in which they'd seek to blow away
the ones from "other teams") –
cuz' whilst the Ulster streets were burning
(motor cars ablaze) –
the I.R.A.'s on hunger strike,
imprisoned in *'The Maze'*!

A famous martyr for the cause,
his name was Bobby Sands –
who started to refuse his food,
for cause of Irish lands.....
But in the British Parliament,
well, Thatcher* - *NOT* impressed –   *6
she reckoned *Sinn Fein* / I.R.A.
were bodies to detest!

When Bobby Sands had passed away,
old Maggie took no pity –
the I.R.A thought *"take revenge –*
let's bomb another city!"
Explosions, killings – on it went,
it seemed, almost - for fun -
but now decided, Thatcher was
their target number ONE.....

The I.R.A. would reach their "peak"
in 1984 –
by wanting to add "Mrs T"
unto their "total score"
The bomb they set in Brighton*   *7
would see several people die –
but missed their target, (Thatcher),
so the chance had passed them by.....

Now Maggie Thatcher got revenge,
(gave Adams little choice) –
when giving broadcast interviews,
she took away his voice!*   *8
Cuz' Irishmen with terror links,
she thought we shouldn't hear –
so he would come on TV, with
an actor's voice, (how queer!)

So after twenty-five long years
(I mean from '69) –
activities of I.R.A.
would go into decline
A full-blown ceasefire was declared
in 1994 –
the end of terror campaigns
and of bombing towns galore.....

Yet peace was interrupted
in the year of '96,
when they set a bomb in Manchester
(return of dirty tricks)
'Twas clear for all, achieving peace
(then keeping nice and stable) -
it needed all opposing parties
talking, round a table.....

Foundations laid by Major
were then built upon by Blair –
so Adams came to No. 10,
the critics cried – *"Not fair!!"*
They claimed that Gerry's terror links
meant blood was on his hands –
and didn't want him shaking hands with Blair,
on English lands!

But –

The *"Good Friday Agreement"*,
this was reached in '98
(it was on the 10th of April,
just to give it's *proper* date!)
To try and list *ALL* details,
would be plain and utter silly!
So here's a list of major points
(without the willy-nilly!):-

> *The I.R.A. would make a pledge*
> *to hand it's weapons in –*
> *(a promise with a deadline),*
> *'else the pact was in the bin*
> *Now in exchange for weapons,*
> *and a lack of things ablaze –*
> *we'd free their 'terror convicts'*
> *(extra early) from 'The Maze'*
>
> *A Parliamentary process*
> *would be set up, making fair*
> *the debating of the issues,*
> *cuz' in fact, they'd power-share.....*

> *This would mean a new "Assembly",*
> *so that everyone could talk –*
> *instead of sitting silently,*
> *all parties in a sulk!*

'Republic's' constitution
would be altered in a way
that would benefit the 'Process',
making harder to betray.....
The Peace Agreement thus proposed
went to a public vote –
the Ulster people gave a "Yes"
they MUSN'T miss the boat!

Yet later on, that very year,
in August '98 –
came a massive bomb in Omagh* *9
which would simply decimate.....
The I.R.A. (direct) it seemed,
this time, was NOT to blame –
instead it was a splinter-group
who'd borrowed half their name* *10

But moving on to present days,
when bombing's rather rare –
the Peace Agreement's held okay,
now there's a better air.....
So fingers crossed, the future's good
and peace is here to stay –
now trusting "Troubles" won't return,
in that, we hope and pray.....

CONCLUSION

Well, Ireland's been 'Republic' now
for near-on, nine decades –
I mean of course, the southern bit,
cuz' Ulster still evades
The I.R.A. has gone away,
(officially, at least) –
through 'Real' and 'Continuity'* *11
the violence ain't increased.....

*In time, they'd hand their weapons in,
(the "proper" I.R.A.) –
despite the doubtful Paisley,
looking on in some dismay.....
Yet in the new Assembly,
well, just look what time would do –
with Paisley, 'leading Minister',
McGuinness – Number Two!!*

*Now things are never perfect,
so we can't play these charades -
there's still a dodgy 'atmos'
when they hold July parades
Though fair to say, in general,
things are better than they were -
these terror acts (from times of old),
so rarely now occur.....*

*And so for now, we end this tale
of Irish history –
yet going back, once more in time,
there's still a mystery.....
Cuz' if old Katy Aragon
had gave her man a son –
would Irish times re-write themselves,
it's future come un-done?*

*IF she had managed to produce
old Henry's next of kin –
then IF he'd not the roving eye
and fancied Anne Boleyn.....
And IF this couple hadn't wished
to run away, elope –
then IF old Henry hadn't sought
an audience with The Pope.....*

*And IF the Pope refrained from knocking
Henry from his perch –
and IF old Henry next, had not
constructed his own Church.....
And IF (like Ireland), England had
remained a Catholic Nation –
would not these countries then avoid
eternal confrontation?*

NO "William of Orange"
and NO "Battle of the Boyne"?
NO 'Sinn Fein' and NO D.U.P.,
NO I.R.A. to join?
But there's no point in speculating,
guessing what we've NOT –
in present times, with peace here,
let's be happy what we've GOT.....

THE STORY GOES ON......

Points marked with an * in this poem refer to:-

*1 H.M. Maze Prison, County Down

*2 Reverend Ian Paisley, of the Democratic Unionist Party (D.U.P.)

*3 D.U.P. = Democratic Unionist Party (as above)

*4 In general, bodies known as *"Republicans"* and/or *"Nationalists"* are
    CATHOLICS – bodies known as *"Loyalists"* or *"Unionists"* are PROTESTANTS

*5 Meaning The D.U.P. (Democratic Unionist Party) and U.U.P. (Ulster Unionist
    Party) on the "Unionist" side – plus "Sinn Fein" and S.D.L.P. (Social
    Democratic Labour Party) on the "Nationalist / Republican" side.
    Also, the I.R.A. splinter groups of "Real I.R.A." and "Continuity I.R.A."

*6 Margaret Thatcher, British (Conservative) Prime-Minister from 1979 to 1990

*7 "Brighton bombing", at the Grand Hotel, Brighton on October 12th 1984

*8 The ban imposed by Margaret Thatcher, that prevented Gerry Adam's voice
    from being broadcast in the media, from 1988 to 1994.

*9 The Omagh Bombing – Omagh, County Tyrone, Northern Ireland on August 15th
    1998.

*10 (The above) carried out by R.I.R.A. ("Real" I.R.A.), who were – and *ARE* –
    opposed to the details of the 'Good Friday Agreement'.

*11 Another reference to the two splinter groups of the former I.R.A., who are
    opposed to the *'Good Friday Agreement'*.

WE SAW A VISION

IN THE DARKNESS OF DESPAIR WE SAW A VISION · WE LIT THE LIGHT OF HOPE · AND IT WAS NOT EXTINGUISHED · IN THE DESERT OF DISCOURAGEMENT WE SAW A VISION · WE PLANTED THE TREE OF VALOUR · AND IT BLOSSOMED ·

IN THE WINTER OF BONDAGE WE SAW A VISION · WE MELTED THE SNOW OF LETHARGY · AND THE RIVER OF RESURRECTION FLOWED FROM IT ·

WE SENT OUR VISION ASWIM LIKE A SWAN ON THE RIVER · THE VISION BECAME A REALITY · WINTER BECAME SUMMER · BONDAGE BECAME FREEDOM · AND THIS WE LEFT TO YOU AS YOUR INHERITANCE ·

O GENERATIONS OF FREEDOM REMEMBER US, THE GENERATIONS OF THE VISION ·

Dublin, September 2010

"How do you solve a problem like Korea?"
Tuesday November 30th 2010

"A classic case of 'One rule for one - another for another?'
Continuing observations in the post – 9/11 period"

There was a man, Saddam Hussein,
he was tyrant bloke -
..although he led a vicious reign
......(his neighbours thought he was a pain,
..........they looked on him with much disdain) –
His weapons were a joke!

Now in these times of terror threat,
some leaders lost the plot!
.."This man has got us in a fret -
......he's storing chemicals, I bet -
..........and hidden them, we'll find 'em yet!"
He didn't have a jot!

The U.N. tried to calm the pack,
to pacify, placate -
.. "We're worried by this info-lack,
......we'll scout around inside Iraq,
..........just hold on, we're reporting back!"
NO CHANCE – they couldn't wait!

Invasion came..........you know the rest,
Saddam, he's come and gone...
..Intelligence? 'twas not the best -
......The *"homework"* had *not* passed the test -
...........These weapons, *Sad'* had not possessed –
Invasion was a con!

Did oil / profit rule the day?
On this, confusion reigned -
..Supporters of the war – *"No way!*
.....*that mad Saddam, he had to pay!*
..........*he had to go, without delay!"*
The question though, remained.....

Spin forward now, two thousand – ten,
Korea's where we're at –
..dictatorship, of *all* the men -
......autocracy, a *Commie* den -
..........most human rights, curtailed in 'gen -
The world begins to chat.....

Now *Nuclear*! They've tried it out,
Atomic, what you will -
..Intelligence? There *isn't* doubt -
......no need to spy and scout about -
..........and every rule, they seem to flout -
..............**they'd slay their neighbours in a rout -**
.................**it seems they will, but stop at nowt –**
The world, it watches, still.....

        So *what d*o they do with a problem like Korea?
                They do **nothing!**

Final conclusions to be drawn:-

1. There is a bad, bad man sat on a *LOT* of oil, who *MAY* have weapons that will pose a serious threat to his neighbours.

What shall we do?

A= *Invade!*

2. There is a highly dubious, tyrannical, dictatorship of a regime in place - with *NO* oil - who are openly showing off and provoking their neighbours with very real and existent *"Weapons of Mass Destruction"* – weapons that threaten not only his neighbours, but world peace.

Shall we invade?

A= Er, no chance mate – best option, sit tight, fingers crossed, close your eyes, hope for the best. *Hopefully*, it'll go away. (Ahem).

"People in Europe" Thursday December 2nd 2010

"England's failed World Cup bid – corruption, corruption, corruption".....

I'm *never* gonna see a World Cup
staged *here* in my life.....
cuz' money rules, corrupted fools
in Europe, running rife......

The E.U. is *corrupt* –
and FIFA is *corrupt* –
- UEFA is *corrupt* –
everyone...**corrupt!**

Why do they bloody *hate* us so,
we ain't done nothing wrong!
Now even *Eurovision*,
they put down our *every* song!

And yet we try to save the world,
sheer billions go abroad –
try telling that to FIFA,
when we *want* something, we're flawed!

Yet everybody *travels* here,
all nations to our shore -
we *only* want a World Cup,
yet they boot us out the door!

Which country was it, rescued *France*
from *German* tenancy?
Yet now those bloody countries
rule the *'Single Currency'*!

We're *hated, hated, hated,*
yes, we English stand alone –
whilst *'nudge-nudge, wink-wink,*
back-hander', then wonder why we moan!

So Putin and his Russian boys
will host in eight years time –
well, let them have the stinking thing,
FIFA's a pantomime!

Been moaning since the news came out,
still moaning now I've supped –
well, I ain't moaning anymore,
the whole thing is **corrupt!**

"Winston's war chant" Thursday December 9th 2010

"A strange distortion of some famous speeches".....

We shall fight them on the oceans
and we'll fight them on the seas –
we'll fight them on the Mersey
and we'll fight them on the Tees
We'll fight them on the beaches
and we'll fight them in the hills –
we'll fight them in the factories,
and fight them in the mills.....

We'll fight them on the landing grounds
and fight them in the air –
we'll fight them on our very streets
and *WON'T* play very fair!
So thus, we *won't* surrender,
oh for sure, we *NEVER* will –
the very thought of "Gerry" here,
it makes me kinda ill!

You ask me *"What's our policy?"*
I answer – *"Waging war!!"*
By ocean, land, and sea, and air –
(up *there*, and on the floor!)
With God in heaven, at our side
he'll give us extra might -
against the Nazi peril,
even on the darkest night!

You ask me *"Winston, what's our aim?"*
I tell you – *"Victory!!"*
(An answer with a single word,
not contradictory).....
Cuz' now I've signed up Roosevelt
he's with us, in our mob –
I say to him *"Give us the tools -
we'll finish off the job!"*

I've offered *nothing* to this House,
but blood, and sweat, and tears –
oh, *not* forgetting 'toil' too,
on this, you've little fears!
Until *one day*, so far away.....
.....no longer will we cower -
and on that day, well, men will say,
"This was their finest hour!"

"Napoleon's Diary"
Saturday December 11th 2010

"I'm Emperor! So 'vive le France!' - we'll knock you on your underpants!" etc, etc.....

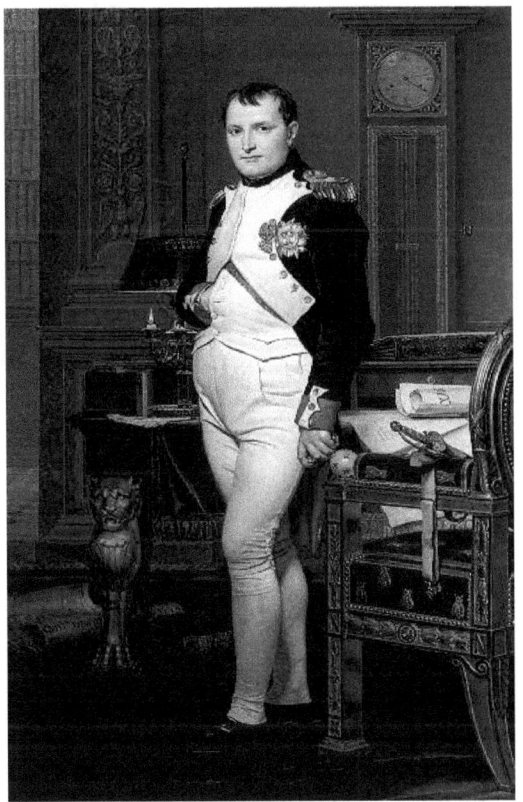

1815.....

Although my frame's a little small,
my armies see me 'walking tall' –
I'm marching off to Waterloo,
campaigns have started up anew!

I'll see my ego thus enhance,
I want more land that's fit for France!
Although I'll win, before the cheers,
well, here's my notes from *other* years:-

Surveying the Sphinx

Boney begins his story:-
Now in the year of '98,
I had this plan to navigate
the dirty Nile, (which really stinks),
but, least I got to see the *'Sphinx'!*
My missus would have loved the 'Med',
I had to leave her home, instead -
and though I couldn't take the kids,
I sent them pics of pyramids!

We're *not* here for vacations though,
of course, the reason's *'money-flow'* -
we French want markets in 'the East',
and better *still*, we'll tame the beast!
By that, I mean our friends, the Brits,
those upper-class, shop-keeping twits -
we need new business, ready-made,
to under-cut their foreign trade!

No sooner had we made some bids,
there's fighting at the Pyramids -
so sorted *that* within a while,
then found the British at the Nile!

I spied old Nelson, *'in the thick'*,
and thought "Don't fancy *this*, I'll pick
a fight, *another* day, you hag" –
and toddled off upon my nag.....

"Battle of the Pyramids"

Corsica seems a long way off,
(my place of birth, you're NOT to scoff!)
I keep it *'mum'*, though it's a wrench,
can't let 'em know that I'm *not* French!
It's just a minor blemish, see,
they like to study ancestry –
I'd tell you more, but there's no room,
this history will now resume.....

In 1800, crossed the Alps,
I wanted some Italian scalps –
believe me not? You English dog!
I took a picture, for my blog:-

(see, picture overleaf)

From Egypt, came to sort this out,
when been away, we've seen a rout -
now taking off Italian hands,
re-claiming back their *latin* lands!

With Nelson busy, thus engaged,
(he's got that Danish fleet *enraged!*)
myself, I've been a busy bee,
more territories have gone to me!
Expanding out, my Empire gains,
we'll have a bigger one than Spain's!
When *will* they crown me - when I'm *dead?*
I'll make *myself* the *'Emp'* instead!

Boney begins to get himself noticed:-
I'm Emperor! So *'vive le France!'*
We'll knock you on your underpants!
And not just *that* - I've Sicily,
(I'm *also* King of Italy!)
Not merely one for taking towns,
I'm after European crowns -
so now I'm sitting on their throne,
the I-ti's sing *'All hail to Bone!'*

In his *'King of Italy'* gown

Next, caught the overnight Express,
so back to France, for games of chess -
my head was measured up for crowns,
while trying out my royal gowns!
And what a party! Where, I think
I had a little much to drink!
I've had a feast, dined at *'The Ritz'*,
now marching off to Austerlitz!

Boney scores his most decisive victory:-
Austerlitz! Now this is bliss,
I won't get better days than this!
Now I'm a genius, it's renowned –
no better tactics have been found!
Those Austro-Russians thought they would
muck me about, they *never* could!
The battle's won, oh what the heck.....
(One day this place will be in *Czech!*)

The Battle of Austerlitz – 1805

Trafalgar's where it all went wrong,
we *knew* the British Navy's strong –
though Villeneuve took us to the dogs,
at least old Nelson's popped his clogs!
Yet *Austerlitz*! Rejoice! Rejoice!
I've sang so much, I've lost my voice –
I'll build an *'Arc de Triomphe'*, pray
my people won't forget this day!

So *onwards*, rolls my war machine!
How many battles have I seen?
Too numerous for me to list
in diaries, so I will resist.....
I wouldn't say it's been a cruise,
well, some you *win*, and some you *lose* –
though NOT time yet, to take my leave,
more master-plans are up my sleeve!

Boney is forced to retreat.....

1812! We've come so far!
Now thought I would upset the *tsar* -
there's *one* thing yet, it's on the map,
a part of Russia, in my lap!
We're closing in on Moscow's town,
but find the skies are sleeting down -
we'll get there yet, before I'm old,
if *only* we survive the cold!

Alas, the winter's snowed us in,
I've *never* felt so perishin'!
Retreating fast, (those Russian smegs!!!)
our frosty tails between our legs!
So now they'll take the p--- from us,
they're cutting records, what a fuss!
I hear them now, composers gay –
'twill make Tchaikovsky rich some day!

"Retreat! Retreat!"

Boney finds that the worm has turned.....

Although I thought *"tis' only blip"*,
how Moscow's made my fortunes dip!
And now I've found *'the worm has turned'*,
my ten year's reign will *end*, I've learned!
NO Emperor – NO *'Vive le France'*!
NO extra lands, NO more advance!
They won't let me negotiate,
I've simply got to *abdicate!*

To Elba! Exiled, on my mule,
they're painting me as quite the fool!
They've *always* called me 'short' – (I'm NOT!) –
say *"Little Boney's gone to pot!"*
Well, let 'em laugh! My wicked foes!
I *could* come back – I guess – suppose?
Lord, tell me that it's *NOT* adieu –
oh, how I need a Waterloo!

LITTLE BONEY GONE TO POT.

He's back.....

I'm back! I've had eight months alone,
and hatched a plan, re-claimed my throne!
I *ALWAYS* said I was *'the Biz'*,
now Boney's *BACK*, it's *not* a swiz!
Refresh the memories in your head,
when starting off this poem said:-
*"I'm marching off to Waterloo,
campaigns have started up anew!"*

I've seen these forty battles won,
what matters *now*, there's only *one* –
the *whole* of Europe hangs on *this*,
it's *'Do or Die'* – Win or a-byss!
Came all this way, risked getting killed,
for fighting in this muddy field –
methinks Belgium's *not* up to scratch,
a horrid place, for such a match!

The Battle of Waterloo - 1815

Boney realizes his mistake.....
Oh bally hell! We need a bus!
Now Wellington's outflanking us!
"Come on, you dogs!! Fight on I say!
I haven't got all bally day!
You think I left my hole for THIS?
You rotten dogs, you take the p---!
Now get stuck in, - you know the crack,
cuz' Welly's got us on the rack!"

"Napoleon's Waterloo"

Yet Boney knows that his final battle is lost.....
"You crazy fools! Now ALL is lost!"
In English jail, I will be tossed -
They'll torture me? Well, I've got *heart* -
they'll *never* pull old *Bone – aparte!*
Ah, now I know what's planned for me,
a prison, in the *southern sea* -
the 'Falklands', or, some land of scrap??
'St Helena??' I'll check the map.....

Boney discovers his fate.....

They've sentenced me to islands scant,
a *dot* that's in the South Atlant' –
I had so many plans, alas,
it's too late now, they'll have to pass.....
I know *this time*, it's over now,
I've left the stage, the final bow –
I spend my long days mournfully,
the genius staring out to sea.....

The genius staring out to sea.....

You'll never know how hard it is,
for me stuck here, still *"full of fizz"* –
my lively mind is in it's prime,
yet gardening's filling up my time.....
My stomach's bad, regrettably,
these vicious pains afflicting me –
I don't deserve this circumstance,
I only did my best for France.....

Six years have I been shunted here,
- no pubs around, can't have a beer!
My stomach pains, worse by the day,
don't know if I will last till May.....
Oh, *if* I had some English quids,
I'd pay to see my wife and kids.....
Yet! *Au revoir!* Here's final breath –
one thing awaits me now......it's death.....

In death.....

Farewell, poor Boney – you were *NEVER* a phoney.....

15th August 1769 – 5th May 1821)

"Mine Campf (Extended) by Aldolph Hittler"
Sunday December 12th 2010

"The little-known EXTENDED diary of monster – a manuscript I found in a bunker during a recent visit to Berlin".....

Adolf Hitler, who wrote a book called *"Mein Kampf"*

<u>1924</u>
It's Tuesday and I'm in a cell –
what rotten luck, I'm sent to jail!
I've not committed massive crime,
it's such a shame, I'm in my prime.....
They've locked me up for my beliefs,
I'm stuck here with these common thiefs –
but I can wait, my name I'll clear,
when *National Socialism's* here!

<u>1925</u>
I'm out at last, my book is wrote,
it strikes a nationalistic note –
to keep alive the German flame
a Nazi Party is the aim.....
I must achieve some power quick,
I'm 35, so time does tick –
let *"League of Nations"* boo and hiss,
I'll shred the terms of Armistice!

Eight years later.....

<u>1933</u>
Promotion's swift, I'm in the door –
I do believe I'm "Chancellor"!
Not YET on top, though I won't bleat –
there's just one bloke now to unseat.....
Von Hindenburg is in my glare,
he DON'T possess the Hittler flair!
It's just a while, I won't relent –
this chance of mine is heaven-sent!

<u>1934</u>
I've hit the top, now life is great –
my Party's IN and I dictate!
If any rebels give me stress,
old Himmler's running my S.S.!
My Josef's propaganda star,
convincing all how great we are!
Our politics stand from the crowd –
no other Parties are allowed!

<u>1935</u>
The Swastika's a logo for
my Nazi Party to adore,
it shows our aims without a doubt
and proves we won't be pushed about!
They all love me, I've many fans –
I'm building all their Autobahns!
At Nuremberg, they think it's odd –
I rant and rave like I'm their god!

<u>1936</u>
They're watching us, as we re-arm
in case we do our neighbours harm –
I'm NOT planning a mass attack,
I only want the Rhineland back!
Sudetenland is what we've missed,
it's topping off my shopping list –
I'm healing up Armistice scars,
and only claiming back what's ours!

1937
To give ourselves the upper hand,
we need extensions to our land –
and so it gave us joy and mirth
by annexing my land of birth....
Vienna's gone the Nazi way,
the Swastika has won the day –
there's acres more I'd like to gain,
but first I'm meeting Chamberlain.....

1938
From bringing us out of arrears,
"Third Reich" will last a thousand years.....
at Nuremberg, I put the case –
I want a German *Master-race*!
Now this will take some foreign treks
and so I thought *"Invade the Czechs!"*
They're calling me "annoying git" –
but after this, I swear – *"that's IT!"*

1939
I didn't want a war as such,
but Neville's pushed me far too much –
I wanted Poland in my bag,
against HIS will, he's such a nag.....
The only thing to do is fight,
shed blood for our Germanic right!
Those British haven't got a clue,
WE'LL take 'em down a peg or two!

1940
My trust in Stalin's water thin,
I'll chuck our pact straight in the bin!
That bloke's a hairy Russian cad,
I'll sort him out at Stalingrad!
At Dunkirk, Brits got up my snout –
they challenged us, then chickened out!
So Churchill's now the man in charge,
like him, his ego's fat and large!

1941

Luftwaffe's up and flying high,
we'll shoot those English out the sky –
it won't be long, they'll call it quits,
cuz' now I've gone and launched a *"Blitz"*!
So every night, these Brits I pound –
they're down the London Underground!
"You will persist, you English dogs –
we'll get you like we got the frogs!"

1942

Campaigns in Russia were a blow,
my lads, they perished in the snow.....
I won't accept it turns the screw,
it only means we've more to do.....
The Russians held us back, but still –
in Egypt, we won't catch a chill,
we're dusted down, we've taken knocks –
but Rommel is my *"Desert Fox"*!

1943

They tried to re-arrange my face
by putting bombs into my case!
I'm worried NOT, though bounders try –
I'll hang these traitors out to dry!
Although we match them pound for pound,
the war is going bad, all round.....
the African Campaign fell flat –
turned out there was a *"Desert Rat"*!

1944

Oh curses! Have I lost my chance?
The Allies have invaded France!
This *"Operation Overlord"*
is something I can ill-afford!
The Allies say the tide has turned,
they think I've got my fingers burned –
though quitting's never in my head,
I sleep uneasy in my bed.....

<u>April 1st 1945</u>
"Keep fighting! It's not over yet!
Cuz' even now, we'll win – I bet!"
(Oh dear, Berlin's under attack –
why don't they keep the Russians back?
I must admit, the war is lost –
we've fought it at a massive cost,
now anonymity's my goal –
you'll find me hiding in my hole!)

<u>April 29th 1945</u>
They've made Benito look a clown,
displayed his body upside down!
No point in hiring me a hearse –
the Russians will be even worse!
Now if that Stalin captures me,
he'll make me look a mockery –
I think I'll marry Eva first,
then make sure Russian dreams are burst!

<u>April 30th 1945</u>
My Eva's *"Mrs Hittler"* now,
I love her, but I can't show how –
there's no point in a honeymoon,
we'll both be dead this afternoon!
Then we shall sleep just like a log
(I've tried the capsules on my dog) –
the Russians are now yards away,
I'd better go, before it's May.....

BANG!!!

<u>Epitaph</u>
"Here lies one mad Germanic berk,
who wanted fame, then went berserk –
'twas in the year of '45,
that he did cease to be alive.....
He murdered millions on the way,
but ended it the coward's way –
he shot a bullet in his head,
so we can laugh, cuz' now he's dead!"

GOOD RIDDANCE!!
1889-1945

"My little-read book" Monday December 13th 2010

"A selection of not-so-quiet Chinese whispers".....

A *"Little Red Book"*, by someone called 'Chairman Mao'.....

"I'm Chairman Mow,
so take a bow –
you want a row ?
Then listen now.....

You take a look
 at my *'Red Book'*
The line I've took(?) –
'I'm NOT a crook!'

I've printed *this*, emphatically
so all of you can think like me –
a little thing that's full of verse,
with *ORDERS* for you to immerse!
I've filled it up with fancy words,
for all you Communistic nerds –
like *'Proletariat'*, et al,
and *"Bourgeoisie"* – *"Das Kapital"*!

With *me* in charge of all you berks
you'll see that socialism works –
now even Stalin was a swiz',
WE'VE GOT A BIGGER WALL THAN HIS!
With me, your leader, at the helm,
we'll see an Oriental Realm –
a newer one, that's *worker*-led
apart from me, cuz' I'm your 'Head'!

I only want the best for us,
Dictatorship, with little fuss –
in theory, we are all the same,
(except myself, cuz' I'm a 'name'!)
The time for 'Revolution's' here!
(A 'Culture' one, so sing it clear):-
*"Now Marx's 'Manifesto's' right,
we'll give the western world a fright!"*

As I'm in need of lucky charms,
I want control of all your farms –
that's *ALL* your peasant lands to me,
it's for the best, I do decree!
I'll risk a million starving souls
through Common Agriculture goals –
'Collectivize' – we'll raise the mood,
that's even if it means no food!

Oh can't you see, this world's bereft
of decent leaders from *'the left'*?
I've done my homework, studied *Marx*,
and memorised his best remarks!
In short, I think you should be proud,
that I'm the *'Chairman'* of the crowd –
it's history! For here's the birth,
the *biggest* Commie zone on earth!

Now if you go in someone's house,
make sure you're sneaky as a mouse –
and thus, please take it on yourself,
to spy a look at their book-shelf!
Then if you find that shelf is bare,
(in other words, my book *ain't* there)
well, don't remain – nor drink or sup -
you leave their home, and grass 'em up!

When houses lack the "Chairman's Verse",
the punishment is death, or *worse* –
I wouldn't like to stand in shoes
of chaps who *know*, yet still refuse.....
By forcing everyone to buy,
there'll be no richer man than I –
I'll swan about, and wear a robe,
the biggest seller on the globe!

And so *conrades*, I do declare,
we'll sing *"The Red Flag"* in *The Square* -
so, *"loud and proud"*, and all that rot,
cuz' if you *don't*, I'll have you shot!
I'm going, I've a dinner date,
there's canine stuff upon my plate –
these *are* my orders, bye for now,
don't disobey – *I'm Chairman Mow!"*

A picture of someone called Mao Tse-tung. Apparently.

"Headley Park (I remember, I remember)"
Tuesday December 21st 2010

"Apologies to the great Thomas Hood – a wicked distortion of my favourite poem by my favourite poet".....

I remember, I remember.....
my house, it had a lawn!
My bedroom window, where the sun
came peeping in at dawn.....
When thought my boyish times would last
forever and a day -
alas, how it's a struggle now,
to keep the lines at bay!

I remember, I remember.....
our home upon the *'Rise'!*
The wooded land around the back,
the stream I'd analyse!
These distant boyhood visions stay,
they'll never disappear -
yet now I'm old, so I am told –
"*stop looking **back**, my dear!*"

I remember, I remember.....
my school at Headley Park!
The jolly conrades in my class,
the Infants was a lark!
Back then, if I had known the things
which I've found out *today* -
would I have ran so happily,
when on the fields of play?

I remember, I remember.....
the lights all going out!
These power-cuts were order of the day –
without a doubt!
When mother lit the candles, well,
it seemed this was the *norm* –
how little did I know back then,
in days of *Tory* storm!

I remember, I remember.....
our garden, and *that* swing!
When sister pushed me to and fro,
I'd *hate* the wretched thing!
But *if* I'd known, how preciously,
these days I'd have to guard -
then maybe I'd have let her push
that extra little hard!

I remember, I remember.....
that year of summer heat!
The *'Parent's Dash'* at Headley Park,
my dad so hard to beat!
These memories, I won't forget,
cuz' in my heart, I'll save –
how sad to think, each day I do –
I'm nearer to the grave.........

That **swing!!!**

"An extra little star"   Friday December 24th 2010

"At Christmas time, remembering loved ones who have passed".....

You left this Earth in peace, and yet
our day seemed gone, our sun was set.....
With days and weeks and years to fill –
mine aching heart to foot the bill

With tortured soul, I looked above
and cried out loud *"Where is my love?"*
Could answer to my question be
so high up in the galaxy?

*.....and my night eye did search the sky,
I saw the twinkling stars on high –
the day you left, when sank the sun,
there shone a little extra one.....*

"Other things"

(Because I wanted to say something in prose!)

"Why I'm Labour"
".....and always will be"

It is in the blood. It really is in the blood. But there is something more than that as well. I don't know what it is, but it pulls you like a magnet.
Yet of course, the genetics have helped.

Because various members of my family have been supporting the Labour Party almost since it's formation in 1900. My great-grandfather started out breaking up old ships for scrap metal at Clevedon around the dawn of the 20th century. When he returned to the city of his birth, Bristol, in 1901, he became a labourer at the city docks. For many years he worked as a crane driver at Princes Wharf, next to the current Industrial Museum. He fought for his country in the First World War and was injured and gassed for the privilege.

But it was actually in the first decade of the Twentieth Century, in the run-up to the Great War, that he came across one Ernie Bevin.

Ernest Bevin had been born in Winford, Somerset, on March 9th 1881 – a date that happened to be only about nine weeks *after* my great-grandfather had been born in Bristol.

It is thought that Bevin started out his working life driving a lemonade wagon around the streets of Bristol.

My great-grandfather would have come across Ernie Bevin for the first time during the early 1900's. By 1910, Bevin had become the secretary of the Bristol branch of the Dockers Union – no doubt, my great-grandfather would have been one of his members. Bevin later became a national organiser for the union. But the two men would continue on to two very separate paths later on in life.

Great-grandfather Hurley continued as a crane-driver and labourer at Bristol docks and fought in the war. He lived in a "two-up, two down" in Bedminster, married and had a large family. He then died (much too early in life) - with severe breathing difficulties brought on by the effects of being gassed in the War – in 1934.

Bevin meanwhile became one of the founding figures, and later, General Secretary of the newly-established Transport and General Workers Union (TGWU), then when Winston Churchill became Prime-Minister and formed an all-Party wartime coalition Government in 1940, Bevin was appointed as

Minister for Labour and National Service, despite not actually having been yet elected as an MP by this time. He then became Foreign Secretary in the much celebrated immediate post-war Labour Government of 1945 – 1951.

It was said that Bevin was the closest confidante of the Labour Prime Minister Clement Attlee. Yet he was *not* a great speaker and never lost his thick West Country accent. He died on April 14th 1951, aged 70 – allegedly, still holding the key to his Ministerial red box.

Apart from my great-grandfather's known involvement with the great Ernie Bevin from way back in the early days of the twentieth century, well, there have been no family stories or legends passed down of Jarrow crusaders, hunger marchers and the like – but loyalty to Labour has always been key. Great-grandfather's daughter Dorothy worked at Wills cigarette factory in Bristol for many years, she was shop steward and fought for workers rights through her position as a formidable, no-nonsense local trade union activist. Grandfather (Dorothy's brother) sweated and toiled for many years as a smelting worker at Avonmouth. He joined the Labour Party and he and his children would be out in all weathers delivering leaflets for the cause, drumming up support for the local candidate.

He despised the Thatcher government and everything it stood for, bemoaning policies that suited the *few* and not the *many* - tax cuts for the rich and the eternal cycle of the mass privatization of British industry at knock-down prices. It remains a source of regret that he never lived to see Labour sweep to power in 1997.

When I was a youngster growing up in the Seventies and Eighties, I would sometimes hear grand-dad discussing politics and ranting about Thatcher with his sons, including my father.

All were pretty much in agreement that she was the worst thing *ever*. I seem to remember some of the wives in the family being (jokingly) critical of the men, commenting that all they ever talked about was football and politics!

But when you are growing up with these things gently simmering in the background, you start to wonder about the world. You wonder why it is that people talk about these things, why they hold the opinions that they do. For example, if they think a certain way, then *why* do they?

At least, that's how it was for me.

This all leaves an impression on you, but it also allows you to develop your own opinions.

When you are watching TV in the early 1980's and you see people rioting and setting fire to cars, as we saw in Toxteth, Brixton and St Pauls, you start to think that there must be something very terribly wrong.

When there are three million people on the dole queues and you see miners fighting police, with their very jobs, livelihoods and communities at stake – (the Labour opposition too weak and divided to do *anything* about it at the polls) - you begin to think *"What the hell is going on in this country?"*

Then it starts to become clear why the people in your family hold the views that they do – these people (as is the case with *me*) - value communities *over* corporations, and Society *over* the Individual.

David Cameron, in 2010, often talks about the "*Big Society*" – yet according to Margaret Thatcher, in a famous speech all those years ago – there was "*no such thing as society*"!

Margaret Thatcher finally lost the plot and went a step too far with her beloved *"Poll Tax"* in 1989, and it became clear from that point onwards that her position was untenable, she no longer had the moral authority to lead this country any further.

But to this day, Thatcher remains the ultimate "marmite" Prime-Minister – you either loved her with a passion, or hated her with a vengeance.

The people around now who continue to sing her praises will claim that Thatcher was arguably the greatest Prime-Minister *ever* and that Britain was known as the *"sick man of Europe"* until her harsh policies "sorted the country out" and began to take effect.....

Those people are entitled to their views, and, at a push – they are even opinions that *could* be PART agreed with – up to a point.

But my answer to that will *always* be, *"At what cost? Was it really worth it?"*

Was it worth the dole queues of three million people, communities - not to mention 'community spirit' - being wiped out forever, British industries down the chute destined never to return, the idea that the Individual is always more important than Society – the selfish attitudes where *"You"* are encouraged to put one over on your neighbour, because *"You"* must aspire to reach the 'top of the tree', WHATEVER the cost to any*one* or any*thing*......(?)

Yet this *is* the legacy that Thatcher has left us, and we are reminded of it whenever we see the *"me, me, me!"* attitudes that are so prevalent within the celebrity culture that we see today, not to mention from within the cult of *"X Factor", "The Apprentice"* and other "elimination" shows of that ilk.....

Thatcherism is still alive and kicking, and very much with us in 2010.....

But this is starting to stray from the point. When Thatcher went, there then followed six and a half years of *'Major sleaze',* before Tony Blair finally got New Labour elected in May 1997 – after eighteen long, long years on the sidelines.....

Believe it or not, I actually think that Labour made many mistakes during it's thirteen years in Government, most notably the disastrous invasion of Iraq and all the things that went with it.

There was clearly too much emphasis on 'spin' and presentation, too much 'man-management' at the very top of the tree, Ministers being sidelined for daring to hold different opinions, and too many un-elected cronies hovering behind Blair, seemingly possessing an alarming capability to influence and even *make decisions* on crucial issues, most notably on foreign affairs.....

But when you actually weigh up all the good and the bad during those thirteen years, it is my genuine belief that when the history books look back on New Labour in power, 1997–2010 – they will remember a government who made genuinely positive changes in people's lives, yes, mostly for the *better* – a government who *cared*, who *gave*.

Yes, Gordon Brown upset the pensioners with the now-infamous 75p rise back in 2000, added to his taxing of their pension funds. But New Labour also *gave back* with free bus passes for the over 60's, free television licenses for the over 75's, the Winter heating allowance and free swimmimg for under-16's and over-60's. Add to this the delivery of a National Minimum Wage, devolving of government powers, a Scottish Parliament and a Welsh Assembly, peace in Northern Ireland via the Good Friday Agreement, record amounts of expenditure poured into key policy areas such as Education and Health – hospital waiting lists slashed, more police officers than *ever* seen before, ditto doctors and nurses.

The 3,600 *Sure Start* centres is possibly the greatest Labour legacy of all, one that everyone in the movement can feel very proud of.

During these times of economic hardship, people also tend to forget that in Gordon Brown, we had arguably one of the most successful Chancellors in British history, who presided over ten years of economic stability before his ill-fated reign as Prime-Minister coincided with the global collapse of the banking system.

However, by the end of the Brown era, the Labour Government was looking jaded and tired, lacking vision and new ideas – it had become very clear that people wanted *change*. But in anyone's book, thirteen years in government is a good innings. Party politics is all about the pendulum that swings from side to side. In May 2010, it swung very much *against* Labour. But it will swing back again.

Under Ed Miliband, we can only hope for a revival in fortunes and ultimately, success in the next election – (whenever it may be) – henceforth, a brighter future than what we've got at the moment.

In order for this to happen, he needs to effectively oppose the Coalition cuts every step of the way, additionally to be able to come up with a credible and workable economic recovery plan of his own.

Fingers crossed.....

But for me, there *are* - and *always have been* - basic values within the Labour movement that I believe I have grown up with, been raised with.

For this reason, I thank god that I have got the parents I *have*, who not only taught me the basics of *right and wrong*, for example that it is wrong to rob, steal, deliberately set out to hurt people, etc, they also raised me with what I would call *'Christian Ethics'* and *'Labour Values'*.

If only I could describe to you what those *'Labour Values'* actually are (!) – and yet I know I've been brought up with them.

The way I have been brought up has influenced me and moulded me – *for better or for worse* – into the person I am today. It has shaped the way I think about things, the way I look at the world, the way I look at politics, the way I see injustice, both in my everyday life, and out there in the wider world.

So I guess it's a big 'Thank you' to my parents for (sometimes inadvertently) making me politically and socially *aware*, to my mum for telling me about the Bible, sending me to Sunday school and teaching me the *"Christian ethics"*, and my dad and *his* family for enlightening me mainly on the political side of things.

I remember as a young boy once asking the question *"Mum, why does Dad support the Labour Party?"*

The answer – *"Because Labour is more for the working man"*.

These days of course, British politics is no longer as clear cut as this simple definition and any description of Labour as a left-wing party for the *'working man'* is not exactly, shall we say, as *accurate* as it once was.

But with the current uneasy alliance of the *'Fib Dems'* in Government with the Tories, it has become absolutely clear without any shadow of a doubt that Labour is now the **only** truly *progressive* party on the centre-left of British politics.

I also believe that the party retains it's basic core values and aspirations

that have *always* been there from it's earliest days, the same values that I've said I have been brought up with, raised with....
I *believe* in it.
Yes, the ideological differences between the two major parties have narrowed and blurred over the last fifteen years. *Yes*, New Labour has been "guilty" of embracing several elements of Thatcherism, courting big business and engaging in part-privatization of the utilities.
But then there is *still* plenty of clear red water between the two parties. We would *never* have seen a National Minimum Wage introduced by any Tory government *ever*, in fact they opposed it's introduction.
I also seem to recall several occasions when they *opposed* all the extra expenditure being poured into public services, when these measures were regularly announced in the (then) Chancellor Gordon Brown's budgets.
Yet the basic *elitism* that is traditionally at the heart of Conservative Party economic policy remains.....
On the other hand, Labour I believe still retains many of it's core aspirations and goals, to reach out and help the most needy and vulnerable in society, ultimately, it strives to help the *many* over the *few*.
Yet supporting the Labour Party for me is *not* about "blind loyalty", or roaring in approval from the rafters at whatever decision they make, nor is it simply about *"Cheering the Reds and booing the Blues, cuz' all the Reds are good and all the Blues are evil"*. It runs a lot *deeper* than that.
And loyalty to Labour is certainly *not* totally unconditional, as the whole sorry Iraq War episode showed me. People aren't perfect, they sometimes make mistakes or take bad decisions *whoever* their political allegiances happen to be with.
But for me, it's *still* all about those aspirations and values, what's in the soul, where their hearts are, what they believe in – and what *I* believe in.
It's why I'll *always* be a Labour man, from now until my dying breath.
I've said that I've been brought up as a *"Labour person"*, and I **have**. I've said that Labour is truly in my genes and my blood, and it **is**.
But I have been an adult for many years now. I have seen a fair old bit of the world and I have made my *own* decisions. I have learned to think for myself, about *who* I am and *what* I believe in.
And for me, it is *still* Labour.....

"How to fairly tax the banks and ease the cuts"

"An F.T.T – Financial Transaction Tax (A 'Robin Hood', or Tobin Tax)"

The *coalition cuts* are now upon us – and apparently we Brits have to face up to the facts and accept them
But why do things have to be like this?
Are the cuts totally *necessary*?
The two main political parties disagree on how best to tackle the budget deficit and National Debt. The Conservatives claim that only deep cuts starting immediately will be able to solve the crisis. Chancellor George Osborne has announced cuts of £81 billion in public spending to be spread over the next four years.
According to Labour, this is both irresponsible and un-necessary. They have a plan to reduce the deficit less dramatically, by easing in staged cutbacks with a view to *halving* the debt over the same four year period.
I believe that the Coalition cuts are completely un-necessary and probably exist for an ulterior purpose to serve their own separate agenda.
I also believe that there are opportunities available to pump billions back into the UK economy and get this country's finances flowing again.
These opportunities appear to be hovering directly beneath the politicians noses – so why aren't the chances being taken?

A Financial Transaction or *Tobin Tax* is hardly a new concept, it has been talked about for many years.
But never has it's potential introduction been as relevant as it is today.
Critics say that the global economic crisis was borne out of the activities of greedy bankers and greedy banking practices.
It is indeed hard to disagree with that point of view. They also claim that as the economic meltdown was *created* by the banks, then it is reasonable to expect that we should all be *bailed out* by the banks – henceforth, the burden should **not** be shouldered by the tax-payer.
The "Robin Hood Tax" – (so-called, because it seeks to take from the rich to help the poor) is a type of Tobin Tax that has been proposed to raise billions for good causes, both at home and abroad.
It is a tiny tax on banks charged at an *average* of only 0.05% on speculative financial transactions (50p on every £1,000 exchanged). **If applied to Sterling it would raise a minimum of £20 billion for the UK.**

"Financial Transactions" – (such as stocks, bonds and currency exchange) - between banks and financial institutions currently pass *TAX-FREE*, which is clearly a massive anomaly.

But the proposed *Robin Hood* levy is a tiny tax on banks, hedge funds and other finance institutions that would raise billions to tackle poverty and climate change, at home and abroad.

A "tiny tax" because it can start as low as 0.005 per cent – and average 0.05 per cent.

But when levied on the *"billions of pounds sloshing round the global finance system every day through transactions such as foreign exchange, derivatives trading and share deals, it can raise hundreds of billions of pounds every year".*

And while international agreement is best, (the G20 springs to mind) it can start right here, right now in the UK.

Revenues from a "Robin Hood Tax" could help stop cuts in crucial public services in the UK, and aid the fight against global poverty and climate change. It's needed NOW because of the financial crisis, frontline services at home – like the NHS and our schools – are under fire.

The people at the *"Robin Hood Tax"* campaign are calling for governments around the world to implement a tax on financial transactions – called the Robin Hood Tax.

It would tax the trade in financial assets such as stocks, bonds and foreign exchange, traded both physically and as derivatives (options, forwards, futures and swaps).

It would cover both those bought and sold on Exchanges and those traded *Over the Counter* (OTC). While OTC trades are technically more difficult to capture, the long-term goal is for all financial transactions to be taxed.

Some of this needs international agreement, but *some,* such as currency transactions can be taxed by individual countries. The UK already taxes share trades with a 0.5 per cent stamp duty. *"Robin Hood"* proposes that it should also tax sterling exchange at 0.005 per cent (5p for every £1,000 exchanged).

How much would a 'Robin Hood Tax' raise?

With a multi-country, G20-style international agreement, up to $400 billion, (or £250bn) globally every year, with the rate of tax varying from 0.5% on stocks to 0.005% on currency transactions. The rate would *average* 0.05%. It is a tiny tax which raises so much because of the sheer volume of transactions.

How would the money be spent?

The "R.H.T." plan is for the $400bn (£250bn) that could be generated by a *global* Robin Hood Tax to be split equally, with $200bn (£125bn) being spent domestically and $200bn (£125bn) spent around the world.

Of the money spent globally, 50% would go towards international development and the other 50% would support developing countries as they adapt to climate change.

The $200bn (£125bn) to be spent domestically would make *"serious inroads into tackling the structural factors that mean more than 13 million people in the UK live in poverty".*

The UK poverty-fighting charities who are supporting the Robin Hood tax have highlighted tackling child poverty, reforming the welfare system, investing in affordable housing and making homes more energy-efficient as the key issues to be tackled by the revenues from the Robin Hood Tax.

The $100bn for international development would help meet the funding shortfall for initiatives such as the Millennium Development Goals and the Global Fund to fight HIV, AIDS, Malaria and Tuberculosis.

All stakeholders would take decisions jointly about collecting and allocating money, with the revenue spent according to developing countries' own poverty reduction priorities – and according to the Paris Principles on Aid Effectiveness.

The $100bn for climate change would *"go a long way towards the $500bn needed annually to help developing countries adapt to and prepare for climate change".*

Funds would be managed by a UN mechanism, to ensure they were allocated fairly and according to each country's particular needs.

Remember, even *without* a multi-country (G20-style) global agreement - by starting the ball rolling *here*, in the U.K., applying a *Robin Hood Tax* to sterling could potentially raise £20 billion *a year* for the British economy. When you compare this figure to Mr Osborne's plans for spending cuts of £81 billion over a four-year period, it doesn't take a genius to work out that, spent wisely, money from an "R.H.T" could potentially wipe out the need for savage cuts on anything like this scale.

For more information, please visit the website of the people who will be able to explain and make things *much* clearer than I:-

http://robinhoodtax.org/

Oh, and just one *last* thing – in case you had forgotten..... P.T.O.

"Poem for the Polish / Poemat dla Polakow"

"A little bit cheeky really, but then I'm only trying to be friendly....."

Poland!

We're greeting you with open arms,
so welcome to our shores!
Feel free to come and go,
now that we've opened up our doors!

We'll see you're well looked after,
we're not keen on being rude –
we're printing Polish newspapers
and storing all your food!

And though you're over-qualified
for many of our jobs –
you're paying in your taxes,
so I think we'll shut our gobs!

I like your Marie Curie
and your Chopin knew a tune -
I always praise Copernicus,
Polanski's no buffoon!

Here's hoping that you prosper,
and we trust you're making friends –
experience of British life
should pay you dividends!

Great!

PHOTOS AND ILLUSTRATIONS

All photos and illustrations (except where indicated*) are copyright-free, and from the Wikimedia Commons website.

commons.wikimedia.org

Main cover sleeve image – "The Matthew passing the Houses of Parliament" – (Houses of Parliament and River Thames by David Castor) – other images including 'The Matthew' and the Clifton Suspension Bridge were added by the author. The author's picture was taken by Laura Davies.

Double-page image spread across opening inner pages – (as above) – in B +W

Back cover sleeve image – "Old mine-shaft at sunset (Daw Mill Colliery, England)" by Chris Sampson

Inner Title page image - "Remains of supposed latrine on the Frome Wall, Bristol" by Bristol Past and Present

Next inner page image - "Bristol Floating Harbour showing the Great Western on the stocks" by Bristol Past and Present

Images from 'Foreward' – "The author, writing poetry on a visit back to Brislington School"* – thanks to Mrs D Blake, and "The Matthew passing the Houses of Parliament" (Houses of Parliament and River Thames by زةوت وسام) – 'The Matthew was added by the author

Images immediately after 'Contents' page - "Rt. Hon David Cameron MP" by Land of Hope and Glory, and "Waste paper basket" by RyGuy.

1. Images From *"Fingers crossed"* – 'The Palace of Westminster, Big Ben and River Thames' by Graeme Maclean - also, 'The River Thames and Houses of Parliament with overcast skies' by Rob, AKA Snowmanradio
2. Images from *"Three cheers for Mr Chatterton"* – 'Thomas Chatterton I' by Unknown, 'Thomas Chatterton II' (Death of Chatterton) by Henry Wallis and 'St Mary Redcliffe Church' by Bristol Past and Present
3. Image from *"Won't you come and dine with me - again (and again)?"*- 'Man dining' by Unknown
4. Image from *"Our Noble Captain"* – 'Rt. Hon. David Cameron MP' by Remy Steinegger, c-o the World Economic Forum'
5. Image from *"Our Noble Deputy"* – 'Rt. Hon. Nick Clegg MP' by The Office of Nick Clegg
6. Image from *"Ireland – her time in rhyme (Part One)"* – 'Brian Boru' c-o IrishGenealogy.com.ar
7. Image from *"Life is s**t at forty"* – 'The author staring out to sea – Garrettstown, nr Kinsale, Co Cork, Republic of Ireland, 2010' by Laura Davies
8. Image from *"A licence to chill"* – 'Old television set' by Rfc1394, AKA Paul Robinson and Simon Cowell/Cheryl Cole by rustyallie, AKA Alison Martin
9. Image from *"Three cheers for Mr Davy"* – 'Humphry Davy" by Unknown
10. Images from *"Lidl Britain"* – 'Rt. Hon. George Osborne MP' by Mholland – 'Rt. Hon. Danny Alexander MP' by Keith Edkins
11. Image from *"I is a British teenager"* – 'Teenager texting' by Olybrius
12. Image from *"Ireland – her time in rhyme (Part Two)"* – 'Old Map of Ireland' c-o The University of Texas, Austin
13. Image from *"A doodle door"* – 'The Rock, Durdle Door, Dorset, England by Gwyn Jones
14. Image from *"Greetings from Dorset (Postcard to a Pensioner)"* – 'Westbay Harbour, Dorset, England' by Aimee Walton
15. Image from *"Charmouth beach"* – 'Charmouth beach, with fossil-hunters' by Kevin Walsh

16. Image from *"Ode to a Nightingale"* – *NOT FROM WIKIMEDIA COMMONS – 'Mary Nightingale, Newsreader', c-o www.dooclip.net
17. Image from *"Ode to a Sky Lark"* – 'Jeff Stelling, Sky Sports News' by Jon Hall, (AKA Ormondroyd)
18. Image from *"Ireland – her time in rhyme (Part Three)"* – 'The Battle of the Boyne, 1690' by Jan Wyck
19. Image from *"A Dublin text message"* - 'River Liffey, Dublin, Ireland' by Thorsten Pohl
20. Image from *"Life in the money factory"* – 'Bank of England printing' by Benj Roberts
21. Image from *"Lady Molyneaux"* – (Woman playing harp) 'Harmony before Matrimony' by James Gillray
22. Image from *"Friday's child"* – 'Drinking' by BocaDorada
23. Image from *"I'm only here to shop!"* – 'Broadmead Shopping Centre, Bristol, England' by Green Lane
24. Images from *"A letter to my leader"* - 'Rt. Hon. Andy Burnham MP' by Jesslane, (AKA The Stage), 'Rt. Hon. David Miliband MP' by U.S. Department of State, (AKA Britishare), 'Rt. Hon. Ed Miliband MP' by Christian Guthier, (AKA Geejo), 'Rt. Hon. Ed Balls MP' by Mark Mozaz Wallis, (AKA Pruneau) and 'Rt. Hon. Diane Abbott MP', by Alex Hilton, (AKA Rwendland)
25. Image from *"Ireland – her time in rhyme (Part Four)"* – 'Irish Emigrants' by Henry Doyle
26. Images from *"Three cheers for Mr Archibald"* – 'Cary Grant' (Screenshot) by Unknown / 'Trailer Screenshot' - and 'Cary Grant' (statue) by Adrian Pingstone
27. Images from *"Ode to the Robin"* – 'A robin' by Ernst Vikne and 'Scrumpy the Robin – Bristol City FC' by Jeremy McNeill
28. Image from *"Ode to our beautiful river"* – 'River Avon at Avonmouth' by Joe D
29. Image from *"Tart FM"* - 'A big love heart' by Bubinator
30. Image from *"The Ten Commandments"* – 'Ten Commandments monument' by Jonathunder
31. Images from *"Ireland – her time in rhyme (Part Five)"* – 'Michael Collins' by Unknown and 'Irish declaration of Independence – Easter Rising, 1916' by jtdirl
32. Images from *"Let's throw an egg at Mr Clegg"* – 'Concert in the Egg' by Jheronimus Bosch and 'Shattered eggshell' by Jahn Henne
33. Images from *"4:25pm (A dream)"* # - 'The Matthew passing the Houses of Parliament', same as FRONT COVER DETAILS – (Houses of Parliament and River Thames by David Castor) –EXCEPT - other images including *'The Matthew'*, the Clifton Suspension Bridge and George Osborne's face in the sky - were added by the author. Also, 'Osborne's portrait blurred into Big Ben's clock-face' was a zoom-in on *Big Ben* as shown in the previous photo , therefore original photo also by David Castor.
34. Image from *"Poem for the Polish/Poemat dla Polakow"* - 'Polish Coat of Arms' by Unknown
35. Image from *'Three cheers for Mr Dirac"* – 'Paul Dirac' by Unknown
36. Images from *"Two Georges"* – 'George Orwell' by the 'Branch of the National Union of Journalists' (B.N.U.J.) – and 'Rt. Hon. George Osborne MP' by Mholland
37. Images from *"The Guy Fawkes Dilemma (1605)"* – 'Guy Fawkes' by George Cruikshank and 'Procession of a Guy (Fawkes)' by Robert Chambers
38. Image from *"Ireland – her time in rhyme (Part Six)"* – 'Bloody Sunday (1972) Mural' by Jerome Sautret, (AKA Zubro)
39. Images from *"There's gonna be a riot!!"* – 'Student protest in London (10/11/10)' by BillyH – and *'Lib Dem April 2010 Student pledge' was a screenshot added by the author.
40. Image from *"Fly the flags, blow the bugles"* – 'Royal Family at Buckingham Palace' by Panhard

41. Images from *"Scandal Days"* – 'Greedy, grasping hands', or 'Greed' by Erich von Stroheim – and 'Many greedy, grasping hands', or 'Greed II' by Erich von Stroheim
42. Images from *"Man's pest friend"* - Main "Holly the Dog" photo c-o the Davies family (Photographer unknown) - second "Holly the Dog" photo by John Davies
43. Images from *"Five have an awfully spiffing time"* - 'Boris Johnson' by Boris Johnson -opening bell at NASDAQ-14Sept2009-3c.jpg' – 'Rt. Hon. David Cameron MP' by Remy Steinegger, c-o the World Economic Forum – 'Ann Widdecombe' by Manchester2k6 – 'Rt. Hon. George Osborne MP' by Mholland -'Rt. Hon. Danny Alexander MP' by Keith Edkins – 'Rt. Hon. Ed Miliband MP' by Off2riorob – 'Rt Hon. Harriet Harman MP' by Steve Punter – and 'Old mine-shaft at night (Daw Mill Colliery, England)' by Chris Sampson
44. Image from *"Cable under the table (A fable)"* – 'Singers in the Egg' by Jheronimus Bosch (Variation on an earlier illustration in No 32, 'Let's throw an egg at Mr Clegg' – also by Jheronimus Bosch)
45. Image from *"The road to Weston Pier"* – 'Weston Pier' by Geof Sheppard
46. Images from *"Ireland – her time in rhyme (Part Seven)"* – 'Martin McGuinness' by 'Scottish and Northern Ireland Ministers' (modifications made by Alison) – 'The Rev and Rt. Hon. Ian Paisley (The Lord Bannside)' by MaxM – 'Gerry Adams' by Domer48 – and 'We saw a vision' (Stone Monument) taken by the author, Dublin, Republic of Ireland in September 2010.
47. Images from *"How do you solve a problem like Korea"* – 'North Korean military with binoculars' by Edward N Johnson - and 'Do not come close or take pictures (North Korean signpost)' by MT13
48. Image from *"People in Europe"* – 'FIFA headquarters in Zurich' by Mcaviglia
49. Image from *"Winston's war chant"* – 'Winston Churchill gives the Victory salute' by British Government
50. Images from *"Napoleon's Diary"* - NAPOLEON BONAPARTE, *'The Emperor in His Study at the Tuileries'* by Jacques-Louis David – 'Viewing the Sphinx' by Jean-Léon Gérôme – 'Battle of the Pyramids' by Francois-Louis-Joseph Watteau – 'Crossing the Alps' by Jacques-Louis David – 'In his *"King of Italy"* robes' by Andrea Appiani – 'Battle of Austerlitz' by François Gérard – 'Retreat from Moscow' by Adolf Northern – 'Exiled to Elba (Caricature)' by George Cruikshank - 'Battle of Waterloo' by Clément-Auguste Andrieux – 'Battle of Waterloo II' by William Sadler – 'The genius staring out to sea (Exiled on St Helena) (x2) by Francois-Joseph Sandmann – and 'On his death-bed' by Horace Vernet
51. Image from *"Mine Campf (Extended) by Aldolph Hittler"* – 'Adolf Hitler' by Slime Turtle
52. Images from *"My little-read book"* – 'Chairman Mao's little Red Book' by Sterilgutassistentin and 'Chairman Mao giant portrait' by Nicholasink
53. Images from *"Headley Park (I remember, I remember)"* – * 'The house where I was born' by Nik White and 'On the swing' *from author's private collection
54. Image from *"An extra little star"* – 'Milky Way (Stars)' by Galactic Explorer

ADDITIONAL POEM – Image from *"Poem for the Polish/Poemat dla Polakow"* (ENGLISH LANGUAGE VERSION) – As with the POLISH LANGUAGE VERSION, 'Polish Coat of Arms' by Unknown

If you are a person who possesses any type of artistic or creative energy, you will know and appreciate the importance of *Influences*. The groups of people who tend to influence these "artistic types" often seem to be characters from all walks of life, family, friends, celebrities, singers, songwriters, people from the world of cinema, literature, science, etc. My long list of *"influential names and blames"* is certainly no different. In fact it's an incredibly, wide-ranging "motley crew" mixture of seemingly un-connected characters, with just *one* thing in common – they have all, in one way or another, (sometimes *small*, sometimes *large*) –

affected me positively as a person, or inspired me somehow, at one time or another;

MY INFLUENCES, AS EVER:-

MOTHER AND FATHER, LAURA DAVIES - ALBARN/COXON/JAMES/ROWNTREE, ROWAN ATKINSON, CLEMENT ATTLEE, TONY BENN, AMBROSE BIERCE, RONALD BINGE, TONY BLAIR, BERRYMAN/BUCKLAND/CHAMPION/MARTIN, CANALETTO, BARBARA CASTLE, JOHN CLEESE, SAMUEL LANGHORNE CLEMENS (MARK TWAIN), RICHARD CURTIS, KENNY DALGLISH, CHARLES DICKENS, ALBERT EINSTEIN, QUEEN ELIZABETH I, BEN ELTON, FRIEDRICH ENGELS, FURUHOLMEN/ HARKET/WAAKTAAR, DAVID LLOYD GEORGE, W E GLADSTONE, WALTER GREENWOOD, PAUL HEATON (+THE LOONY-LEFT LYRICS OF THE HOUSEMARTINS), AUDREY HEPBURN, THOMAS HOOD, JOHN HURLEY, GORAN IVANISEVIC, DAVID JASON, FRANZ KAFKA, KEVIN KEEGAN, NEIL KINNOCK, THE LABOUR PARTY, D H LAWRENCE, EDWARD LEAR, JOHN LENNON, MARTIN LUTHER KING, KARL MARX, JAMES MAXTON, STEVE MCQUEEN, WARREN MITCHELL, MICHAEL MOORE, STEVEN PATRICK MORRISSEY, GEORGE ORWELL, ROBERT OWEN, THOMAS PAINE, SIR GREGORY PARSLOE-PARSLOE (MATCHINGHAM HALL, SHROPSHIRE). WILLIAM PEARCE, MICHAEL POWELL, EMERIC PRESSBURGER, SIMON SCHAMA, BILL SHANKLY, the late, lamented JOHN SMITH MP, OSCAR WILDE, BRUCE WILLIS, HAROLD WILSON, P G WODEHOUSE. NOT FORGETTING SEVEN OUT OF ELEVEN *'DOCTORS'* – BILL HARTNELL, PAT TROUGHTON, JON PERTWEE, TOM BAKER, PETER DAVISON, CHRIS ECCLESTON AND DAVID TENNANT.

Thanks again to Bob Isaacs, who has seen a bit of life and knows what it's all about.
Thanks also to Nik White - photographer supreme - whose talents I have only recently discovered. Please look out for his excellent new website, which was about to hit the Internet just as this book went to print.
Thanks again to Erwin Wozniak for translating my nonsense into Polish,
and thanks to all personnel at *"Paradise Heights"*.

Cheers all!

WEBSITES YOU MAY BE INTERESTED IN:-

http://www.darrenhurleysparadisepoems.com

http://stores.lulu.com/darrenhurley

http://www.lulu.com/

http://robinhoodtax.org/

http://www.waronwant.org/

http://www2.labour.org.uk/

The date of the poem titled *"4:25pm (A dream)"* was 20/10/10 – the afternoon that George Osborne announced his Comprehensive Spending Review in the House of Commons – in other words, the official unveiling of *'The Cuts'*.....

Now dry your eyes.....and blow your nose –
this *Paradise* is soon to close.........

"Thou Widdecombe! Ye sexy minx!
I'm loving you to bits!
I only watched that *"Strictly"*
cuz' I thought you'd do the splits!
Thou graceful girl, so full of bounce -
God bless your every pound!
Ye take no heed of jealous jibes
which say you're fat and round!"

To be continued......(Unfortunately!) –

so watch this space.....

(Because once is *instigation*.....
twice is *repetition*.....
thrice is a *tradition!)*

The older gear - *still* available.....while stocks last... (ahem)

www.ingramcontent.com/pod-product-compliance
Ingram Content Group UK Ltd.
Pitfield, Milton Keynes, MK11 3LW, UK
UKHW022231230426
12048UKWH00016BA/1189